Lonely 🌐 planet

POCKET
ORLANDO
& WALT DISNEY WORLD® RESORT

TOP EXPERIENCES • LOCAL LIFE

FIONN DAVENPORT

Contents

Plan Your Trip 4

Minnie Mouse plush toys
CRAIG RUSSELL/SHUTTERSTOCK ©

Welcome to Orlando & Walt Disney World® Resort

Boost your adrenaline on a hair-raising ride, hop on the Hogwarts Express, and meet Elsa and Anna from *Frozen*. In Orlando, the Theme Park Capital of the World, there's plenty to explore – from theme-park thrills to gardens and galleries – and you're set for the trip of a lifetime.

COVID-19

We have re-checked every business in this book before publication to ensure that it is still open after the COVID-19 outbreak. However, the economic and social impacts of COVID-19 will continue to be felt long after the outbreak has been contained, and many businesses, services and events referenced in this guide may experience ongoing restrictions. Some businesses may be temporarily closed, have changed their opening hours and services, or require bookings; some unfortunately could have closed permanently. We suggest you check with venues before visiting for the latest information.

Orlando cityscape
SEAN PAVONE/SHUTTERSTOCK ©

Top Experiences

Celebrate 50 years of Disney (p36)

Watch fireworks explode at Disney Enchantment (p52)

Get lost in Pandora – The World of Avatar (p84)

Make magical memories in Diagon Alley (p94)

Explore the Galaxy's Edge with Star Wars (p68)

Wander the Wizarding World of Harry Potter at Hogsmeade (p106)

Learn about rocket launches at the Kennedy Space Center (p144)

See the wonders built from bricks at Legoland® Florida Resort (p148)

Escape to elegant Winter Park (p150)

Dining Out

One thing Orlando has no shortage of is places to eat – 75 million visitors can get pretty hungry. The parks have a mix of fast-food and gourmet experiences, International Drive has a concentration of midrange and high-end chains, while Downtown and Winter Park have thriving dining scenes focused on fusion and field-to-fork cuisine.

In the Parks

Walt Disney World® and Universal Orlando Resort feed the multitudes with a dizzying selection of themed restaurants and take-away outlets. Most of it is (tasty) fast-food fare, but there are some exceptional choices throughout, especially in Epcot's World Showcase and Universal's CityWalk. The higher-end resort hotels also have some fine-dining restaurants.

International Drive

The 5-mile stretch of Sand Lake Rd from I-4 (at Whole Foods) west to Apopka-Vineland Rd, and including Dr Phillips Blvd, is known as Restaurant Row. Here you'll find a concentration of restaurants and high-end chains more popular with locals than tourists, with everything from wine bars to cigar bars, sushi to burgers. I-Drive is also home to the world's biggest McDonald's.

Downtown Orlando

Dozens of Korean, Vietnamese, Chinese and other Asian eateries cluster along several blocks of Orlando's Mills 50 neighborhood. Winter Park has a great selection of farm-to-fork eateries, as does Downtown, particularly around W Church St.

Best of Walt Disney World®

50's Prime Time Café
Classic dishes served in a '50s-style home setting. (p72)

HENDRICKSON PHOTOGRAPHY/SHUTTERSTOCK ©

Be Our Guest Dinner in the Beast's castle (from *Beauty and the Beast*) is a gourmet affair. (p62)

Monsieur Paul Jérôme Bocuse's imprimatur is on this exceptional French restaurant. (p79)

Boma A menu focused on broadly African cuisine is the best of fine dining, buffet-style. (p43)

Best of Universal Orlando Resort

Mel's Drive-In Classic '50s diner. (p101)

Three Broomsticks Harry Potter–inspired school lunches. (pictured above left; p112)

Leaky Cauldron Dine in Hogwarts style. (p100)

Best Downtown & Winter Park

Pig Floyd's Urban Barbakoa Delicious BBQ with exotic touches. (p137)

Kabooki Sushi Best sushi in town. (p137)

Maxine's on Shine Neighborhood joint with superb food. (p137)

Best for Families

'Ohana All-you-can-eat buffet with a Polynesian theme. (p44)

Paradiso 37 Latin American feasts. (pictured above; p46)

T-Rex Cafe Kid-oriented spot with surprisingly good dishes. (p45)

Mythos Restaurant Dine in an underwater grotto. (p113)

Mobile Ordering

A great way to avoid long lines is to use mobile ordering, available in Walt Disney World® and Universal Orlando Resort through their respective apps. Pre-order (and pay for) your meal and then let the restaurant know when you've arrived to pick it up. Not all restaurants are included.

Bar Open

With so many vacationers around, it's hardly surprising that Orlando likes to enjoy itself. For the majority of visitors, I-Drive is where most of the action takes place, but the best bars and clubs are spread throughout Downtown.

KENT PHILLIPS/DISNEY ©

Themed Bars

Orlando *loves* a good theme bar. Downtown has a bunch of bars designed to look like Prohibition-era speak-easies, and you'll also find bars where it's Christmas year-round and Halloween every day: a living hell if you actually had to endure it every day, but great fun for a night or two. In the parks, you can enjoy a drink like you're a character in *Star Wars* or a Harry Potter novel, grab a beer in Homer Simpson's favorite bar or explore spirits and cocktails from around the world at Epcot's World Showcase.

In the Parks

Disney Springs and the much smaller Disney's BoardWalk are the designated drinking (and entertainment and shopping) districts at Walt Disney World®, but you'll find bars and sometimes live music at most Disney resorts and within the theme parks. Magic Kingdom sells beer and wine only, available at the more formal, sit-down restaurants. There's a bigger selection of bars and nightlife at Universal's CityWalk.

MATT STROSHANE/DISNEY ©

Best Downtown

Mathers Social Gathering
Superb craft cocktails in a
speakeasy setting. (p139)

Cocktails & Screams It's
Halloween every night in this
bar that celebrates all things
horror and Gothic. (p140)

Bösendorfer Lounge
Supremely elegant hotel bar
whose name derives from
the rare grand piano that
has pride of place. (p140)

Hanson's Shoe Repair
Old-school cocktails, a daily
changing password to get
in...is this Chicago in 1927?
(p140)

Best in Disney

Jock Lindsay's Wait...the
pilot from *Raiders of the Lost
Ark* opened a bar in Disney?
(pictured above; p48)

Belle Vue Room Get away
from the mayhem in this
quiet 2nd-floor bar designed
to look and feel like a living
room. (p48)

La Cava del Tequila With
220 types of tequila, the
perfect margarita awaits at
this Epcot gem. (p81)

Oga's Cantina Go full *Star
Wars* at this themed bar in
Disney's Hollywood Studios.
(p69)

Best in Universal Orlando Resort

Moe's Tavern Who *doesn't*
want to have a drink in
Homer's favorite watering
hole? (pictured above left;
p102)

Hog's Head Pub Never
mind the Butterbeer: this
Harry Potter–themed pub
serves real beer too. (p113)

Duff Brewery Waterside bar
serving Homer's favorite
brew. (p103)

Chez Alcatraz San
Francisco–themed bar in the
middle of Universal Studios.
(p103)

Roller Coasters

From the mildest to the wildest ride, surrendering to the thrill of a roller coaster is the ultimate Orlando experience. Everyone has their favorite, whether it's an old-school wooden coaster that clickety-clacks around a hairpin turn, or a high-tech hyper coaster that delivers heart-pounding g-forces and stomach-turning drops.

Height Requirements

While the majority of coasters at Walt Disney World® are open to everyone, some have a minimum height requirement, usually ranging from 36in to 48in depending on the intensity of the ride. Most of the coasters at Universal Orlando Resort and SeaWorld have minimum height restrictions, and some – mostly hyper coasters that invert – have size restrictions. Either way, a height line and a seat at the entrance will determine whether you can ride or not.

Coaster Types

Wooden and steel: the two main types of roller coaster are defined not by the car, but by the track. Wooden roller coasters run on tracks braced by wooden crossties and diagonal support beams. Although the range of movement is limited and they're considered tamer, wooden coasters are designed to sway a little, which makes for a unique effect and an added thrill.

Steel coasters run on long steel tubes that allow for a much broader range of versatility and movement. Besides a traditional sit-down coaster, there are inverted coasters, suspended coasters and flying coasters.

Where Should I Ride?

Here's some tips on how to make the most of your roller coaster experience:

Front row Ride in the front row – not only will you see everything coming, but the blast of wind can enhance the thrills.

Back row These seats will guarantee better airtime over hills and the biggest impact of g-force.

Middle rows Best for coaster newbies or anyone who wants to ride but is a little nervous.

Night rides The less you can see, the more your distance perception dwindles and the faster the ride feels. Trust us, and try it for yourself.

Best Indoor Coasters

Revenge of the Mummy Coaster that twists through the darkness. (p97)

Rock 'n' Roller Coaster Starring Aerosmith Zero to 57mph – in three seconds flat. (p71)

Space Mountain Magic Kingdom's most popular ride is this indoor trip through the star-studded galaxies. (p61)

Best for Speed

Mako SeaWorld's (and Orlando's) fastest coaster has some serious 'hang' time. (p125)

Incredible Hulk Coaster A burst of speed and lots of turns. (pictured; p109)

Hollywood Rip Ride Rockit A steep drop, lots of twists and 65mph. (p97)

Manta Flying coaster at SeaWorld where you ride face down. (p125)

Kraken Your feet dangle free in this steel, floor-less SeaWorld coaster. (p125)

Best for Families

Big Thunder Mountain Railroad Mild Magic Kingdom favorite. (p60).

Hagrid's Magical Creatures Motorbike Adventure Quick, but not scary, with a couple of surprises. (p107)

Peter Pan's Flight Gorgeous indoor flight through Neverland. (p57)

E.T. Adventure Classic Universal ride with the family-friendly alien. (p99)

Under 10s

COURTESY OF LEGOLAND® FLORIDA RESORT ©

While Orlando offers something for all ages, it really knows how to take care of the under 10s. They're young enough to marvel that dreams really do come true, to giggle with delight at a hug from Snow White and stand awed by magical happenings, but they're also old enough for many of the rides, especially at Walt Disney World®.

Go Wild!

Even if you're coming for Orlando's theme parks, consider taking some time away from their spinning wheels of eye candy to explore the parks and lakes in and around the city. You don't have to be a hard-core outdoor enthusiast or go very far to take a peek into Florida's wilder side, which makes it perfect for kids – within an hour of Walt Disney World®, you can be paddling calm waters past alligators, turtles and heron, or tubing down a spring-fed river.

Making Food Fun

Sure, you'll find chicken nuggets and burgers, lemonade and cola in all the parks, but the real fun is in the whimsical theming of the parks' food and drink. The Flaming Moe in Universal Studio's Springfield bubbles with smoke, tiny 'fish eggs' settle on the bottom of Diagon Alley's Fishy Green Ale, and Seuss' fruity Moose Juice comes fresh or frozen. And at Disney, even the butter on your breakfast tray comes stamped with Mickey Mouse.

Best Classic Experiences

Peter Pan's Flight Gentle flight through the story and over London. (p57)

Mad Tea Party Quintessential Disney spinning. (p60)

Festival of Fantasy Daytime parade with current favorites from animations and more. (p65)

Pirates of the Caribbean Slow cruise through the world of pirates. (p59)

Mickey's PhilharMagic A 3D jaunt into classic Disney movies. (pictured above right; p65)

Fantasmic Light show starring Mickey as the Sorcerer's Apprentice. (p73)

it's a small world A classic slow water journey with that song. (p57)

DISNEY ©

Best Coasters

Big Thunder Mountain Railroad Gentle coaster through the Wild West. (p60)

Flight of the Hippogriff Listen for Fang's barks and don't forget to bow to Buckbeak. (p107)

Expedition Everest Zip backwards to escape the Yeti. (p87)

Seven Dwarfs Mine Train Heigh-ho it's off through Fantasyland we go. (p58)

Best TV- & Movie-Based Rides

Star Tours: The Adventures Continue Take a virtual reality tour through the galaxy with Chewbacca and Han Solo. (p72)

Despicable Me: Minion Mayhem Minions, minions and more minions in marvellous 3D simulation. (p98)

Toy Story Midway Mania! Ride-through video game. (p72)

Na'vi River Journey Slow journey through beautiful Pandora. (p85)

Frozen Ever After Journey to Elsa's ice palace. (p78)

Best Areas for Under 5s

Seuss Landing Charmingly whimsical Seuss-themed rides, play area and story performance. (p110)

Fantasyland Toddler-perfect storybook rides, 3-D Donald Duck movie and princesses everywhere. (p57)

Legoland Smaller, less crowded and rides without any trace of scary special effects. (pictured above left; p148)

Motion Simulator Rides

Also known as 'dark rides' as they operate in an enclosed space, the best motion simulator rides are made up of a compelling narrative, good interactive (4D) elements and cutting-edge video technology that makes you feel like you're in the middle of the action. Note: the combined effect can lead some to feel motion sickness.

Best Immersive Experiences

Avatar: Flight of Passage It actually feels like you're flying on a banshee. (p85)

Simpsons Ride A trip to Krusty the Clown's amusement park turns wild. (p97)

Harry Potter & the Forbidden Journey Wind through Hogwarts and fly over the school in a quidditch match. (p107)

Star Wars: Rise of the Resistance The virtual ride is only part of this extraordinary experience. (p69)

The Void Star Wars or Wreck-it-Ralph: either way, it's brilliant VR. (p42)

Amazing Adventures of Spider-Man A 4D adventure with the webbed wonder. (pictured; p109)

Skull Island: Reign of Kong Stunning high-tech 3D visuals make this one of the great rides. (p111)

Twilight Zone Tower of Terror It just *feels* like the elevator is dropping. (p71)

Best for Families

Despicable Me: Minion Mayhem Become one of Gru's minions in this marvelously silly 3D simulation. (p98)

Soarin' Around the World Brilliantly rendered bird's-eye trip around the globe. (p77)

Millennium Falcon: Smuggler's Run Board the *Millennium Falcon* for the world's most immersive video game. (p69)

Toy Story Midway Mania! Discover the inside of Andy's toy box in brilliant 3D. (p72)

DINOSAUR A dinosaur-inspired multisensory simulated ride into prehistoric jungles. (p88)

Race Through New York Starring Jimmy Fallon G-rated ride with superb simulated effects. (p98)

Water Rides

© DISNEY

Orlando is rarely cold and in summer, it gets very, very hot – and humid. Water parks aren't just a theme-park choice, but often an absolute necessity. Walt Disney World® has two, and Universal Orlando Resort and SeaWorld both have one each, but even within their respective theme parks is a fine selection of splash rides.

Orlando's Water Parks

Walt Disney World® has two water parks, Typhoon Lagoon (p42) and Blizzard Beach (p43), both of which have a good selection of slides, tube rides and lazy rivers. But for overall experience, the best is Universal's Volcano Bay (p115).

Best Thrill Rides

Kala & Tai Nui Serpentine Body Slides Twin slides that hurtle down a volcano. (p117)

Ko'okiri Body Plunge The tallest free-fall drop slide in Orlando. (p117)

Krakatau Aqua Coaster A high-tech water coaster. (p117)

Crush 'n' Gusher Typhoon Lagoon's biggest thrill is this water coaster. (p43)

Summit Plummet Drop 12 stories through this slide. (p43)

Best for Families

Splash Mountain Animatronic animals and a classic watery splash. (pictured; p61)

Jurassic Park River Adventure Dinosaur-themed journey. (p111)

Dudley Do-Right's Ripsaw Falls Water ride silliness with a 75ft plunge. (p111)

Popeye & Bluto's Bilge-Rat Barges White-water rafting guaranteed to get you soaked. (p111)

Character Interactions

Folks of all ages pay a lot of money and spend hours in line to interact with their favorite character. The good news is there's plenty of opportunities to do so, from meet-and-greets and photo ops to character meals and interactive shows. You'll need to plan carefully and well in advance (especially for Disney) – these are very popular.

Meeting Characters

Disney's character meets are a big part of the experience – whether it's Winnie-the-Pooh, Donald Duck, Elsa, or Mickey and Minnie, who are Disney royalty – so check www.disneyworld.com. Characters roaming Universal Orlando Resort include anyone/anything from the likes of Curious George and SpongeBob SquarePants to the cast of characters from *Despicable Me* (pictured), *Shrek,* and Dr Seuss books.

Best for Interactive Performances

Finding Nemo: the Musical Magnificent puppets on stage and down the aisles transform *Finding Nemo* into a Broadway-style musical. (p89)

Festival of the Lion King Interactive singing and dancing performance in Animal Kingdom. (p87)

Best Dining with Characters

Grand Floridian Resort Buffet breakfast with Winnie-the-Pooh, Mary Poppins and Alice in Wonderland. (p167)

Chef Mickey's Dine with Goofy, Donald and the gang. (p47)

Akershus Royal Banquet Norwegian-inspired feast with Disney princesses. (p81)

Cinderella's Royal Table Dine in the castle with your host, Cinderella. (p63)

Feast with Marvel's Finest Buffet meal where you meet Captain America, Spider-Man, Wolverine, Storm and Rogue. (p113)

Despicable Me Character Breakfast Gru, Margo and the minions join you for breakfast. (p113)

For Free

There are a handful of free highlights in and around Orlando. In addition, you can enjoy street energy in the tourist hubs of the theme parks: CityWalk (Universal Orlando), Disney's Board-Walk (near Epcot) and Disney Springs. All are open to the public and there's no entry fee. Parking is free at Disney Springs and after 6pm at CityWalk.

JEFF GREENBERG/EDUCATION IMAGES/UNIVERSAL IMAGES GROUP VIA GETTY IMAGES ©

Free Wine Tastings

The daily tours and tastings at **Lakeridge Vinery & Vineyards** (☏ 352-394-8627; www.lakeridgewinery.com; 19239 US-27, Clermont; ⏱10am-5pm Mon-Sat, 11am-5pm Sun) are completely free. The 45-minute experience includes a 15-minute video followed by a tour of the production area and a peek at the expanse of this 127-acre vineyard, Florida's largest. It also hosts a free music series throughout the year, as well as a free open house during the holidays. It's about 25 miles northwest of downtown Orlando, just off Florida's Turnpike in the townland of Clermont.

Best Free Stuff

Orlando Farmers Market Crafts, food and an outdoor beer garden. (p143)

Winter Park Farmers' Market Neighborhood market in a historic train depot. (p153)

Best for Culture

Cornell Fine Arts Museum Top-class art gallery with a selection of work from all around the world. (pictured; p151)

Hannibal Square Heritage Center Small museum focusing on African American history in Winter Park. (p151)

Thursday Gallery Hop

On the third Thursday of every month there's an art and culture crawl in downtown Orlando, with live music and monthly themes at various venues – see www.orlandoslice.com for more details.

Treasure Hunt

A common Orlando scene is tourists buying an extra suitcase or two, just to fit all of the purchases they've made. Orlando has some of America's largest outlet malls, and we dare you to run the theme-park retail gauntlet with your kids and resist the overwhelming urge to stock up on a sizable quantity of branded memorabilia.

INSPIRED BY MAPS/SHUTTERSTOCK ©

Outlet Shopping

International Drive has a bunch of factory outlet stores, mostly clustered at its northeast end near Universal Orlando Resort. Here you'll also find one of two malls owned by Premium Outlets, which has 180 stores; the other is closer to Disney, at the intersection of I-4, US525 and International Drive.

Theme Park Retail

You can't walk 100yd in any theme park without coming across a retail opportunity, but for serious shopping, Disney Springs has a big range of well-known brand stores, as well as the world's biggest Disney store. Universal's CityWalk isn't as focused on shopping, but there's a large Universal store there.

Best Outlet Shopping

Orlando Premium Outlets – International Drive Huge outlet mall with 180 different stores representing most well-known brands. (p127)

Best Theme Park Stores

Ollivander's Buying a wand here is like you're actually a character in a Harry Potter book. (pictured; p95)

Lego Imagination Center Who knew you could do such amazing things with Lego? (p49)

World of Disney The world's biggest Disney store: if this shop doesn't have it, it just hasn't been made. (p49)

Once Upon a Toy One of the very best toy stores in all of America has everything, old and new. (p49)

Bibbidi Bobbidi Boutique Transform your child into a princess or a knight at this lovely store inside Magic Kingdom's Cinderella Castle (p65)

Golf

With more than 60 golf courses spread throughout the area, Orlando is something of a golfer's paradise. There are a dozen or so championship courses, including a fine selection at Walt Disney World®. Call individual golf courses for information on club rental and twilight rates.

SAM GREENWOOD/GETTY IMAGES ©

Disney Courses

Walt Disney World® is home to five 18-hole golf courses – three of which have featured on the PGA Tour schedule in the past – as well as a nine-hole course and a couple of miniature golf tracks. Check out **Walt Disney World® Golf** (📞 407-939-4653; www. golfwdw.com; from $40) for all information, including bookings.

Best Courses

Disney's Magnolia Golf Course (1950 W Magnolia Palm Dr, Disney's Grand Floridian Resort & Spa; per round from $49)

The longest of Disney's five golf courses, this one-time regular on the PGA Tour is notable for its testing length and handsome magnolia trees.

Disney's Lake Buena Vista Golf Course (1960 Broadway, Walt Disney World®; per round from $45) A championship golf course, designed in classic country-club style, with lakes and pine forests. Test out your approach shot – a major feature is its elevated bunkered greens.

Bay Hill Golf Club (pictured; 📞 407-876-2429; www.bayhill.com; 9000 Bay Hill Blvd; rates connected to room rates at Bay Hill Club & Lodge) The private host course of the prestigious Arnold Palmer Invitational on the PGA Tour is, despite

its name, flat as a pancake. Most try to emulate the pros and play the 18 holes that make up the Champion/ Challenger course, but you can replace either with the 9-hole Charger course. Open to members and hotel guests only.

Disney's Oak Trail Golf Course (1950 W Magnolia Palm Dr, Disney's Grand Floridian Resort & Spa; per round from $49) Family-friendly, nine-hole walking course.

Disney's Palm Golf Course (1950 W Magnolia Palm Dr, Disney's Grand Floridian Resort & Spa; per round from $40) This Arnold Palmer–designed, 18-hole championship course is one of Disney's most pictur-esque, with palm trees, lakes and sloping greens.

Under the Radar

JILLIAN CAIN PHOTOGRAPHY/SHUTTERSTOCK ©

With more than 75 million annual visitors all in town for pretty much the same thing, it's not hard to break away from the lure of the theme parks and explore other parts of Orlando.

Downtown

Orlando's relatively undiscovered Downtown is one of the city's most beautiful districts, even if few people know about it. A new addition in 2022 is **Steinmetz Hall** at the **Dr Phillips Center for the Performing Arts** (www.drphillipscenter.org; 445 S Magnolia Ave), a 1700-seat multiform auditorium reckoned to be one of the world's most acoustically perfect spaces. Another addition is **ART²** (Art Squared; Cnr Orange Ave & Robinson St), an urban park built around a two-story shipping container that includes a cafe, art gallery, stage and digital wall. And when you're done, you can retreat to **Maxine's on Shine** (p137) for a romantic late-night meal; this much-loved restaurant near Lake Eola added a large terrace during the pandemic that has become one of Downtown's favorite spots for a bite.

Leu Gardens

A soothing antidote to the colorful chaos of the theme parks is a visit to the stunning Leu Gardens (pictured p134) in Loch Haven Park. This 50-acre oasis surrounding a 19th-century mansion has tropical plants from all over the world – one of the benefits of Orlando's specific climate. Bring a picnic and time your visit to coincide with one of the many events, including movie nights in summer.

Culture

Orlando a cultural destination? You betcha it is, but you have to look in the right places. After all, Orlandoans might appreciate the impact the theme parks have on the local economy, but for the most part they live their lives separately from them. Which means they look elsewhere for creative distractions, usually Downtown and in Winter Park.

EDUCATION IMAGES/UNIVERSAL IMAGES GROUP VIA GETTY IMAGES ©

Museums

Orlando's collection of fine art and history museums isn't huge, but the few it has are of a pretty high standard, and in a couple of cases, genuinely world-class.

Art

Florida's most compelling native art movement is represented by the Florida Highwaymen, a group of 26 African American artists including Alfred Hair, AE Backus, Harold Newton and Mary Ann Carroll that, between the 1950s and 1980s, painted the underdeveloped Florida landscapes in a style of refined naturalism. They got their name because as artists working outside the mainstream, they mostly sold their work by the side of the road.

Best Museums

Charles Hosmer Morse Museum of American Art Exquisite collection of Tiffany glass (pictured; p151)

Hannibal Square Heritage Center The culture and history of African Americans in Winter Park (p151)

Kennedy Space Center America's space exploration HQ tells the story of NASA in fabulous detail. (p144)

Best Galleries

Orlando Museum of Art Fine collection of American art, especially work by the Florida Highwaymen. (p135)

Mennello Museum of American Art Top-class collection of work by Earl Cunningham. (p134)

Cornell Fine Arts Museum European Old Masters and other art from around the world, including Latin America. (p151)

Four Perfect Days

Day 1

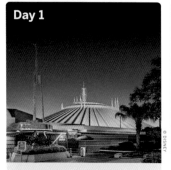

© DISNEY

Get to **Magic Kingdom** (p51) early for the opening ceremony. Hop on **Peter Pan's Flight** (p57) before the lines get long. Scurry over to **Splash Mountain** (p61), zip across to **Space Mountain** (pictured above; p61), and then to **Pirates of the Caribbean** (p59) before the lines swell.

Dine with Minnie Mouse at **Chef Mickey's** (p47), then take in **Mickey's PhilharMagic** (p65) before hitting other rides. Wander Main St, USA (p61) and try for nighttime return-times at the FastPass+ kiosk.

Catch a boat to Disney's Polynesian Village Resort for kebabs at **'Ohana** (p44). Hop on the monorail back to Magic Kingdom in time for the **Disney Enchantment** (p52) nighttime spectacular.

Day 2

Dawn entry to **Disney's Hollywood Studios** (p67) should be rewarded with a boarding pass for Rise of the Resistance in **Star Wars: Galaxy's Edge** (p68). Good planning means using Fast-Pass+ to go on **Millennium Falcon: Smuggler's Run** (p69) before exploring the rest of the Black Spire Outpost.

After lunch at **50's Prime Time Café** (p72), ride **Rock 'n' Roller Coaster Starring Aerosmith** (p71). Hightail it over to **Animal Kingdom** (pictured above; p83) and use your FastPass+ reservation for **Avatar: Flight of Passage** (p85).

Transfer to **Epcot** (p75), where your World Showcase dinner reservation awaits – try **Tutto Gusto** (p80) or **Monsieur Paul** (p79).

Day 3

Go early to **Universal Studios** (p93) and make a beeline for the **Wizarding World of Harry Potter – Diagon Alley** (p94); guests of Universal Orlando resort hotels can get into Harry Potter attractions one hour before everyone else. Ride **Escape from Gringotts** (p95), then hop on the **Hogwarts Express** (p95) to **Hogsmeade** (p106).

Ride **Hagrid's Magical Creatures Motorbike Adventure** (pictured above; p107) before having lunch at **Three Broomsticks** (p112). Pick your coaster – perhaps the **Incredible Hulk Coaster** (p109) in Islands of Adventure, then, a Hogwarts Express later, **Hollywood Rip Ride Rockit** (p97) in Universal Studios.

End the day with a Duff Beer from **Moe's Tavern** (p102).

Day 4

Spend the morning in **Volcano Bay** (pictured above; p115), testing slides, flumes and lazy rivers – try both the **Kala & Tai Nui Serpentine Body Slides** (p117) and the **Krakatau Aqua Coaster** (p117) if you dare!

In the late afternoon head to **Winter Park** (p150) and visit the Tiffany masterpieces in the **Charles Hosmer Morse Museum of American Art** (p151).

Sip a self-serve wine flight at **Wine Room** (p151), before indulging in some of the city's best field-to-fork dining at **Prato** (p152), where you should try to snag a sidewalk table. Even if you're not staying there, pop into the gorgeous **Alfond Inn** (p153) for a cocktail after dinner or go all out with a Downtown Orlando bar crawl (p130).

Need to Know

For detailed information, see Survival Guide (p155)

Cell Phones
Foreign phones that operate on tri- or quad-band frequencies will work in the USA. Otherwise, purchase inexpensive cell phones with a pay-as-you-go plan when you arrive.

Currency
US dollar ($)

Language
English

Money
ATMs are widely available. Major credit cards are widely accepted.

Time
Eastern Standard Time (GMT minus five hours)

Tipping
Tipping is expected: 15% to 20% of bill; $1 to $2 per drink; 10% to 15% of taxi fare.

Visas
Required for all international visitors except those eligible for the ESTA program.

Daily Budget

Budget: Less than $200
Walt Disney World® value resort room for four people: $110
Self-catering and cheap eats: $40–60
Seven-day bus pass: $16

Midrange: $200–400
Theme-park accommodations for four: $200
Multiday theme-park ticket: $50–120
Car rental per week: $300–400

Top end: More than $400
Luxury or easy-theme-park-access accommodations for four: $400-plus
Theater ticket: $40–80
Themed Disney dining or top-end restaurant: $90–160

Advance Planning

Three months before Snag a table at Disney character, themed and high-end restaurants.

Two months before Book your hotel, purchase theme-park tickets and reserve Disney FastPass+ attractions (if not staying on site, reserve 30 days in advance).

Three weeks before Check hotel prices and make changes if necessary – cancellation policies are generous and prices fluctuate dramatically. Buy theater tickets.

Arriving in Orlando

✈ From Orlando International Airport

Disney's Magical Express (📞866-599-0951; www.disneyworld.com) Complimentary luxury transport to Walt Disney World® resort hotels (book in advance).

Taxi Twenty-five to 35 minutes ($55 to $70) to Lake Buena Vista and Universal Orlando Resort area.

✈ From Orlando Sanford International Airport

Taxi Around 40 minutes to the Universal Orlando Resort area ($85 to $100) and one hour to Lake Buena Vista ($120 to $130).

🚗 Towncar Transport

Orlando Airport Towncar (📞800-532-8563; www.orlandoairporttowncar.com) and **Legacy Towncar of Orlando** (📞888-939-8227; www.legacytowncar.com) operate out of both airports; fares around $100 to parks and downtown.

Getting Around

🚗 Car

Rentals at airports, some hotels and Disney's **Car Care Center** (📞407-824-3470; www.disneyworld.com; 1000 Car Care Dr; ⏰7am-7pm Mon-Fri, to 4pm Sat, to 3pm Sun).

🚝 Theme Park Transportation

Disney and Universal offer complimentary bus and boat transportation. Disney monorail connects two parks, some Disney hotels and the **Transportation & Ticket Center** (www.disneyworld.com; Walt Disney World®; Magic Kingdom parking $25).

🚕 Taxi

Cabs outside theme parks, Disney Springs and hotels; ride-share services are cheaper than taxis.

🚌 Bus

LYMMO (www.golynx.com; free; ⏰6am-10:45pm Mon-Fri, from 10am Sat, 10am-10pm Sun) circles downtown Orlando for free.

Walt Disney World® Resort Regions

Magic Kingdom (p51)
With Cinderella's Castle, it's a small world, Splash Mountain, Main Street, USA, and Mickey's PhilharMagic, this is Disney for Disney purists.

Walt Disney World® (p35)
Over 40 sq miles of theme parks, water parks, golf courses, entertainment districts and dozens of hotels: a whole world of Mickey!

Epcot (p75)
A quirky take on the future with a handful of rides and the country-specific attractions of World Showcase.

Disney Enchantment

Walt Disney World®

Pandora – The World of Avatar

Star Wars: Galaxy's Edge

Animal Kingdom (p83)
Animal-themed park set in 'Africa', with the added bonus of the extraordinary Pandora – The World of Avatar.

Disney's Hollywood Studios (p67)
Hollywood nostalgia and 21st-century energy combine with plenty of Jedi action for avid *Star Wars* fans.

Explore Walt Disney World® Resort

Walt Disney World® is indeed a network: the area covers 42 sq miles and includes four separate (walled) theme parks and two water parks, all connected by a complicated system of monorail, boats and buses, and intersected by highways and roads. Attractions, primarily in the form of rides, character interactions, movies and shows, are spread out among the six parks, resort hotels and, to a lesser extent, two entertainment districts.

Walt Disney World®

Cinderella Castle. Space Ship Earth. Mickey Mouse. And now, a whole land dedicated to Star Wars. Spread across 42 sq miles, Walt Disney World® isn't just the world's most famous theme park, but a powerful cultural icon that represents the innocence of childhood and the promise of a magically fun time.

The Short List

◦ **Disney Enchantment (p52)** *Projections, fireworks and the power of dreams light up Cinderella Castle and Main Street, USA.*

◦ **Star Wars: Galaxy's Edge (p68)** *Travel to a galaxy far, far away and immerse yourself in the Star Wars universe.*

◦ **Splash Mountain (p61)** *Join Br'er Rabbit and Br'er Fox for a thrilling, wet ride.*

◦ **Avatar: Flight of Passage (p85)** *Ride a banshee and soar through a marvellously rendered, beautiful 3D landscape.*

◦ **Frozen Ever After (p78)** *Travel to Elsa's ice palace aboard a dragon-headed boat while singing songs from Frozen.*

Getting There & Around

🚉 From the airport, Disney hotels or Transportation & Ticket Center (TTC).

🚝 From Epcot, Magic Kingdom and some hotels.

⛴ From Magic Kingdom, Disney's Hollywood Studios, Epcot and TTC.

🚗 South of Downtown, 25 minutes. Park at TTC.

Region Map on p40

Walt Disney World® theme-park entrance OCTAVIO JONES/GETTY IMAGES ©

Top Experience 📷
Celebrate 50 Years of Disney

It's been quite a ride in the half century since Walt Disney World® first threw open its doors on October 1, 1971. As far-reaching as Walt Disney's imagination was, not even he could have guessed that the park would become not just the most visited tourist attraction in the world, but part of the very fabric of American culture.

◉ **MAP P40, D5**

📞 407-939-5277

www.disneyworld.com

Lake Buena Vista, outside Orlando

daily rates vary, from around $109, see website for discount packages & tickets up to 10 days

The Beginnings

When Disneyland opened in southern California in 1955, it fundamentally transformed the concept of theme parks. Walt Disney, however, was irritated at the hotels and concessions that had sprung up around the park in a manner he felt was entirely parasitic. Plus, visitor data showed that only 2% of park guests came from east of the Mississippi.

In 1964, after a secret four-year search, Walt Disney bought 27,000 acres of swamp, field and woodland in central Florida. He paid an average of $200 an acre, but once the cat was out of the bag that he was the buyer, the price shot up to $80,000.

Disney's vision was to create a family vacation destination wherein he could control every aspect – hotels, restaurants, parking and transportation. It wouldn't just be a theme park, but a 'city of tomorrow,' a planned community where people would live and work. At the formal announcement of the plans on November 15, 1965 (nicknamed 'D-Day for Orlando'), Governor Hayden Burns called the date the most significant in the history of Florida.

Alas, Disney would never see his vision fulfilled. Just a year later, he died of lung cancer, forcing his brother Roy to come out of retirement to take over responsibility for development. Roy barely survived the opening, dying of a brain hemorrhage two months later.

The Parks

Walt Disney World's Magic Kingdom – with Walt's full name added as a tribute – opened on October 23, 1971, with the total cost of the project around $400 million. In the first two years, the park drew 20 million visitors a year, transforming the quiet citrus town of Orlando into the fastest-growing city in the state, the 'Action Center of Florida.'

★ **Opening Hours**

o Opening hours change day to day within any given month. Typical hours are 8am or 9am to between 6pm and 10pm.

o At least one park has early opening for Walt Disney World® hotel guests only – these 'Magic Hours' are a major perk of staying at a Disney resort hotel.

★ **Key Telephone Numbers**

Walt Disney World®
(📠 407-939-5277)

Disney Dining
(📠 407-939-3463)

Activities
(📠 407-939-7529)

Tours
(📠 407-939-8687)

Lost and Found
(📠 407-824-4245)

Epcot – the park that best represented Walt's 'vision of tomorrow' – opened in 1982, followed by Disney-MGM Studios (now Disney's Hollywood Studios) and Typhoon Lagoon in 1989. Blizzard Beach opened in 1995 and, three years later, Animal Kingdom. All the while, around the parks were opening more than a dozen resorts, a campground and a vast array of recreational facilities, including golf courses. Disney Springs first opened in 1975 as the Lake Buena Vista Shopping Village.

The impact of Walt Disney World® cannot be underestimated. It transformed central Florida, and the arrival of SeaWorld in 1973 and Universal Orlando in 1990 cemented Orlando's new status as the Theme Capital of the World. But Walt Disney World® has changed the very nature of theme parks, from a passing attraction into an all-encompassing hermetic experience driven by constant development and innovation. In 2020 Disney was flexing its considerable creative and technological muscle to prepare for its 50th anniversary in 2021, but if the first 50 years are any indication, that effort will continue well into its second half-century of life.

Mickey and Minnie

Top Tips for a Successful Disney Vacation

Buy tickets that cover more days than you think you'll need It's less expensive per day, and it gives you the freedom to break up time at the theme parks with downtime in the pool or at low-key attractions beyond theme-park gates.

Stay at a Walt Disney World® resort hotel While it's tempting to save money by staying elsewhere, the value of staying at a Walt Disney World® resort lies in the convenience offered.

Download the Disney app 'My Disney Experience' You can make reservations, reserve FastPass+ attractions, and view listings, programs and your own schedule.

Take advantage of 'My Disney Experience' Reserve your three FastPass+ attractions per day (www.disneyworld.com) up to 60 days in advance (30 days for nonresort guests).

Stock up on snacks You'll save the irritation of waiting in line for average, overpriced food.

Arrive at the park at least 30 minutes before gates open Don't window-shop or dawdle – just march quickly to the rides and then kick back for the afternoon. Factor in the time to get here from the Transportation & Ticket Center (this can take up to an hour).

Program 'Disney Dining' into your cell phone While you'll want to make some plans well in advance, once you have a sense of where you'll be at mealtime, call ☎ 407-939-3463 to make reservations at table-service restaurants.

Think about both accommodations and transportation When booking accommodations it's worth considering your transport options. All Disney resorts offer bus transportation, but those offering boat and monorail transportation are far more convenient (and, except for camping at Fort Wilderness, more expensive).

Go with the flow This is about managing expectations. If you build up the idea that your child will definitely hug Belle in a so-called 'character meet,' only to see the line is ridiculous, then recalibrate. Suggest initially that you're going to spot, rather than visit, a character. Believe us, you'll end up spotting them in parades or by chance. In addition to your three FastPass+ experiences, you can head to any of the activities listed in the daily schedule/map.

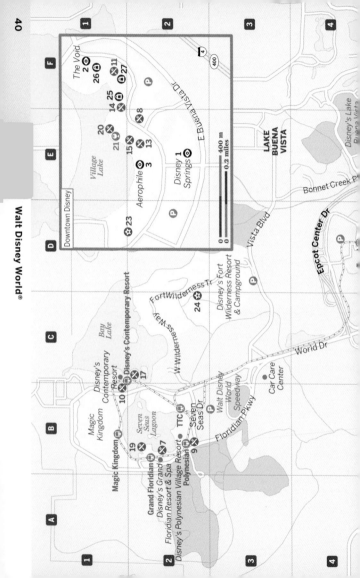

Walt Disney World®

Downtown Disney

The Void 2
26
11
27
14 25
8
20
21
15 13
Aerophile 3
Disney 1
Springs
23

E Buena Vista Dr

LAKE
BUENA
VISTA

Bonnet Creek P

Epcot Center Dr

Vista Blvd

0   400 m
0   0.2 miles

Fort Wilderness Tr
Disney's Fort
Wilderness Resort
& Campground
24

W Wilderness Way

World Dr

Bay Lake
Disney's Contemporary Resort
Disney's Contemporary
Resort
10
17

Car Care
Center

Magic Kingdom
Seven
Seas
Lagoon
19
7
Grand Floridian
Disney's Grand
Floridian Resort & Spa
Disney's Polynesian Village Resort
Polynesian
9

TTC
Seven
Seas Dr

Walt Disney
World
Speedway

Floridian Pkwy

Disney's Lake
Buena Vista

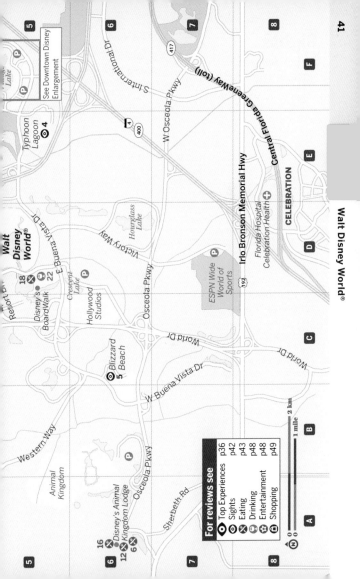

Walt Disney World®

See Downtown Disney Enlargement

Typhoon Lagoon ◉ 4

Walt Disney World®

S International Dr

W Osceola Pkwy

417

400

4

Central Florida Greenway (toll)

Irlo Bronson Memorial Hwy

Florida Hospital Celebration Health ✚

CELEBRATION

192

ESPN Wide World of Sports Ⓟ

Hourglass Lake

Victory Way

Crescent Lake

Resort Blvd

18 ✕ 22 ✕

Disney's BoardWalk

E Buena Vista Dr

Hollywood Studios

Osceola Pkwy

World Dr

World Dr

◉ Blizzard 5 Beach

W Buena Vista Dr

Western Way

Osceola Pkwy

Ⓟ

Animal Kingdom

Disney's Animal Kingdom Lodge

16 ✕
12 ✕ 6 ◉

Sherbeth Rd

For reviews see
◉ Top Experiences   p36
◉ Sights   p42
✕ Eating   p43
🍸 Drinking   p48
☆ Entertainment   p48
🛍 Shopping   p49

1 mile

2 km

N

A   B   C   D   E   F

5   6   7   8

Sights

Disney Springs
AREA

1 ⊙ MAP P40, E2

The primary entertainment district in Walt Disney World® – with shops, restaurants and bars, live music and a movie theater – stretches along the waterfront. You can take buses from Disney resorts to Disney Springs, and a few hotels offer boat transport to the area, but you cannot take Disney transport from here to any theme or water parks. Admission and parking is free. (☏407-939-6244; www.disneyworld. com; 1490 E Buena Vista Dr, Walt Disney World®; ⏰8:30am-2am; 🚌Disney, 🚢Disney, 🚌Lynx 50)

Understanding the Four Parks

By far the most visited park is **Magic Kingdom** (p51), which embodies more than anywhere else the magical spirit of Disney. **Epcot** (p75) is currently undergoing a substantial revamp – one of the largest transformations in its history. **Disney's Hollywood Studios** (p67) has been transformed by the opening of Star Wars: Galaxy's Edge. The safari-like **Animal Kingdom** (p83), the youngest of the four, is least like a traditional theme park, but is where you'll find Pandora – The World of Avatar. See individual chapters for details of each.

The Void
AMUSEMENT PARK

2 ⊙ MAP P40, F1

Don a pack and VR goggles and lose yourself in your choice of two adventures. In **Star Wars: Secrets of the Empire** you're disguised as a stormtrooper and have to solve and blast your way to survival. In **Ralph Breaks VR**, you join Wreck-it-Ralph and Vanellope von Schweetz to sneak into the internet's coolest video games – and get involved in a food fight. As good a VR experience as you'll find anywhere. (www.thevoid.com; 1732 E Buena Vista Dr, Disney Springs; $40; ⏰10am-11pm Sun-Thu, to 11:30pm Fri & Sat; 🚌Disney, 🚢Disney, 🚌Lynx 50)

Aerophile
RIDE

3 ⊙ MAP P40, E2

Guests climb onboard the basket of this massive tethered gas balloon and ascend 400ft into the air for 360-degree views. Between 8:30am and 10am there's a special for $10 per person. (☏407-939-7529; www.disneyworld.com; 1620 East Buena Vista Dr, Disney Springs; adult/child $20/15; ⏰8:30am-midnight; 🚌Disney, 🚢Disney, 🚌Lynx 50)

Typhoon Lagoon
WATER PARK

4 ⊙ MAP P40, E5

An abundance of palm trees, a zero-entry pool with a white sandy beach, high-speed slides and the best wave pool in Orlando make this one of the most beautiful water parks in Florida. The most thrilling slide of them all is the

Crush 'n' Gusher water coaster, but little ones will love floating along **Castaway Creek** and splashing at **Ketchakiddee Creek**. (📞407-560-4120, 407-939-5277; www.disneyworld.com; 1145 Buena Vista Dr, Walt Disney World®; adult/child $73/63, prices vary daily; ⏰hours vary; 🚌Disney)

Blizzard Beach   WATER PARK

🎯 ⊙ MAP P40, C6

The newer of Disney's two water parks, themed as a melted Swiss ski resort complete with a ski lift, Blizzard Beach is the 1980s Vegas Strip hotel to Typhoon Lagoon's Bellagio. At its center sits **Mt Gushmore**, home to **Summit Plummet**, a 12-story free-fall slide with speeds up to 55mph. (📞407-560-3400, 407-939-5277; www.disneyworld.com; 1534 Blizzard Beach Dr, Walt Disney World®; adult/child $73/63, incl in Water Park Fun & More with Magic Your Way theme park ticket; ⏰hours vary; 🚌Disney)

Eating

The following dining options are either located at Disney Springs or within Disney-themed hotels outside the parks. See the individual parks' eating sections for more dining options.

Boma   BUFFET $$$

🎯 🍴 MAP P40, A6

Several steps above Disney's usual buffet options, this African-inspired eatery offers wood-roasted meats, interesting soups such as coconut

---

Embark on a Disney Tour 🔍

Disney offers all kinds of guided **tours** (📞407-939-8687, VIP tours 📞407-560-4033; www.disneyworld.com; Walt Disney World®; prices vary) and specialty experiences, including the **Wild Africa Trek** private safari and backstage Disney tours. One of the most popular is the five-hour **Keys to the Kingdom** (📞407-939-8687; www.disneyworld.com; Magic Kingdom; tours $99, theme-park admission required; ⏰8am, 8:30am, 9am & 9:30am) tour that takes you behind the scenes at Magic Kingdom.

For the ultimate in hassle-free touring, with front-of-the-line access to attractions and insider information on the park and its history, consider a **VIP tour** ($400 to $600 per hour per group of up to 10 people).

---

curried chicken and plenty of salads. Handsomely furnished with dark woods, decorated with African art and tapestries, and flanked by garden-view windows on one side, Boma offers not only good food but unusually calm and pleasant surrounds. (📞407-938-4744, 407-939-3463; www.disneyworld.com; 2901 Osceola Pkwy, Disney's Animal Kingdom Lodge; adult/child breakfast $38/20, dinner $49/27; ⏰7:30-11am & 5-9:30pm; 📶♿; 🚌Disney)

Victoria & Albert's AMERICAN $$$

7 ⊗ MAP P40, B2

With one sitting per evening and a prix-fixe menu as the only choice (vegetarian option available), this opulent Victorian-themed dining room provides one of the poshest meals in all of Florida. Everything is beautifully prepared, and desserts by pastry chef Kristine Farmer are divine. You must reserve directly (not through the Disney Dining number) and well in advance. (📞407-939-3862; www.victoria-alberts.com; 4401 Floridian Way, Disney's Grand Floridian Resort; prix-fixe from $295; ⏰5:30-9pm; 🤵; 🚌Disney, ⛴Disney, 🚝Disney)

Frontera Cocina MEXICAN $$

8 ⊗ MAP P40, E2

A smart, trendy version of modern Mexico where, thanks to Chef Rick Bayless, corn, chili and salsa are whipped up into contemporary tastes in a delightfully light, bright and bustling environment. A pleasant change from some Southern flavors. Fun margarita-filled happy hours, too. (📞407-560-9197; www.fronteracocina.com; 1620 East Buena Vista Dr, Disney Springs; mains $24-38; ⏰11am-10pm Sun-Wed, to 10:45pm Thu-Sat; 🚌Disney, ⛴Disney, 🚌Lynx 50)

'Ohana POLYNESIAN $$$

9 ⊗ MAP P40, B2

The Polynesian's signature restaurant evokes a South Pacific feel with rock-art animals, a huge oak-burning grill cooking up massive kebabs of meat, and demonstrations of hula and limbo dancing, plus other Polynesian-themed shenanigans. The only thing on the menu is the all-you-can-eat family-style kebabs and veggies, slid off skewers directly onto the giant wok-like platters on the table.

Breakfast is a Lilo and Stitch character meal. (📞407-939-3463; www.disneyworld.com; 1600 Seven Seas Dr, Disney's Polynesian Village Resort; feast adult/child breakfast $25/14, dinner $55/35; ⏰7:30am-noon & 3:30-10pm; 🤵; 🚌Disney, ⛴Disney)

California Grill AMERICAN $$$

10 ⊗ MAP P40, B1

Disney's signature gourmet restaurant has commanding rooftop views of the Magic Kingdom fireworks, which for many is reason enough to bag a table. But the clincher is the superb menu, with everything from quirky sushi to triple-cheesed flatbreads. Reservations should be made well in advance (up to 180 days for peak season). (📞407-939-3463; www.disneyworld.com; 4600 World Dr, Disney's Contemporary Resort; mains $37-52; ⏰5-10pm; 🤵; 🚌Disney, ⛴Disney, 🚝Disney)

Ghiradelli Soda Fountain & Chocolate Shop ICE CREAM $

11 ⊗ MAP P40, F1

Decadent ice-cream concoctions involving entire chocolate bars blended into milkshakes. (www.

Disney Springs (p42)

disneyworld.com; 1620 East Buena Vista Dr, Disney Springs; ice cream $4-9; ⊙9:30am-11:30pm Sun-Thu, to midnight Fri & Sat; P 🛜 👫; 🚌Disney, 🚢Disney, 🚌Lynx 50)

Sanaa
SOUTH INDIAN $$

12 ✖ MAP P40, A6

Lovely cafe with savanna views – giraffes, ostriches and zebras graze outside the window. You almost forget you're in Florida, but, hey, that's Disney. The food is South Indian – try the slow-cooked tandoori chicken, ribs, lamb or shrimp; the delicious salad sampler with tasty watermelon, cucumber and fennel salad; and a mango margarita. (📞407-939-3463; www.disneyworld.com; 3701 Osceola Pkwy, Kidani Village, Disney's Animal Kingdom Lodge; mains $15-25; ⊙11:30am-3pm & 5-9:30pm; 🖊👫; 🚌Disney)

Chef Art Smith's Homecomin'
AMERICAN $$

13 ✖ MAP P40, E2

Chef Art Smith is a local celebrity chef, so local fans love his Floridian farm-to-fork, old-style-meets-modern flavors. We're talkin' fried chicken, shrimp and grits, and pork barbecue. (📞407-560-0100; www.disneyworld.com; Disney Springs; mains $22-31; ⊙11am-11pm; 🚌Disney, 🚢Disney, 🚌Lynx 50)

T-Rex Cafe
AMERICAN $$

14 ✖ MAP P40, F1

Over-the-top multisensory overload, with massive autotronic dinosaurs, volcanoes erupting, light shows and meteor showers every 15 minutes. The menu features Woolly Mammoth Chicken, Caveman Punch and Chocolate Extinction – you get the idea. Kids will love it and the food is better than you might expect. (📞407-828-8739; www.disneyworld.com; 1620 East Buena Vista Dr, Disney Springs; mains $18-22; ⏱11am-11pm Sun-Thu, to midnight Fri & Sat; 🅿🛜🚻; 🚌Disney, ⛴Disney, 🚌Lynx 50)

Paradiso 37 SOUTH AMERICAN $$$

15 ❌ MAP P40, E2

With a menu representing 37 countries of the Americas, this contemporary waterfront spot is one of Disney Springs' best bets. It's very family-friendly, but nighttime has live music, a fiesta atmosphere – and 75 types of tequila. Plan accordingly. Call directly for reservations – it often has more flexibility and openings than Disney Dining. (📞407-934-3700; www.paradiso37.com; 1620 East Buena Vista Dr, Disney Springs; mains $31-43; ⏱11am-11pm Sun-Thu, to midnight Fri & Sat; 🅿🛜🚻; 🚌Disney, ⛴Disney, 🚌Lynx 50)

Jiko – The Cooking Place AFRICAN $$$

16 ❌ MAP P40, A6

Excellent food, with plenty of grains, vegetables and creative twists, a tiny bar, and rich African surrounds make this a Disney favorite for both quality and theming. You can relax with a glass of wine on the hotel's back deck, alongside the giraffes and other African beasts. For a

Boathouse

less-expensive option, enjoy an appetizer at the bar. Swing by for dinner, or at least a cocktail, after a day at Animal Kingdom. (📞407-938-4733; www.disneyworld. com; 2901 Osceola Pkwy, Disney's Animal Kingdom Lodge; mains $35-60; ⏰5:30-10pm; 🍴👶; �monorail Disney)

Chef Mickey's   AMERICAN $$$

17 ✖ MAP P40, C2

Nothing says Walt Disney World® Resort more than Mickey Mouse and the monorail, so what better way to start your classic Disney day than a buffet breakfast with Mickey Mouse, Minnie Mouse, Pluto, Donald Duck and Goofy under the roar of the monorail. Head to Chef Mickey's for an early breakfast, then hop on the monorail and get to Magic Kingdom when the gates open. (📞407-939-3463; www.disneyworld.com; 4600 World Dr, Disney's Contemporary Resort; adult/child from $50/33; ⏰7-11:15am, 11:30am-2:30pm & 5-9:30pm)

Flying Fish   SEAFOOD $$$

18 ✖ MAP P40, D5

Specializing in complicated and innovative seafood dishes, Flying Fish is one of the best upscale dining spots at Disney. It's a slick, contemporary spot with a modern ocean theme (note the bubble chandeliers). Be sure to reserve ahead. Kids' meals are significantly cheaper (from $14 to $23). (📞407-939-3463, 407-939-2359; www. disneyworld.com; Disney's BoardWalk; mains $33-59; ⏰5-9:30pm; 🍴👶; 🚇Disney)

Narcoossee's   SEAFOOD $$$

19 ✖ MAP P40, B2

Muted waterfront dining on the boat dock at the Grand Floridian makes a convenient, relaxing and lovely respite if you've been at Magic Kingdom for the afternoon and want to return after dinner for the fireworks. The menu is dominated by all kinds of California-influenced seafood, but there are also a couple of succulent steaks. (📞407-939-3463; www.disneyworld. com; 4401 Floridian Way, Disney's Grand Floridian Resort; mains $41-70; ⏰5-9:30pm; 👶; 🚇Disney, 🚢Disney, 🚇Disney)

Boathouse   SEAFOOD $$

20 ✖ MAP P40, E1

All kinds of seafood fills the menu at this upscale waterfront spot, as well as classic craft cocktails and a good wine list (that showcases American wines). Nightly music entertains you well into the morning. After dinner and drinks, head off for a spin and a float in a genuine **amphicar** (up to 3 people 25min $125; ⏰10am-10pm). (📞407-939-2628; www.theboathouseorlando. com; 1620 East Buena Vista Dr, Disney Springs; mains $21-34; ⏰11am-1:30am)

Drinking

Jock Lindsay's BAR

21 MAP P40, E1

According to, er...'old' Disney folk-lore, Jock (the pilot in *Raiders of the Lost Ark*) 'arrived here in 1938 while chasing down a mythology-based tip in central Florida.' He liked the natural springs and lush terrain, and so bought some land. His hangar (his home base) became popular for world travelers and locals...and here you now are.

Disney's Boardwalk

Far less harried and crowded than Disney Springs, the quarter-mile-long **Disney's BoardWalk** (Map p40, D5; ☎407-939-5277; www.disneyworld.com; 2101 Epcot Resorts Blvd, Walt Disney World®; 🖥Disney, 🚗Disney) area across from Epcot and along Crescent Lake echoes waterfront boardwalks of turn-of-the-century New England seaside resorts. On Thursday to Saturday evenings, magicians, jugglers and musicians give a festive vibe, and there are a handful of good restaurants and bars. Pick up a doughnut or cute li'l Mickey Mouse cakes at the bakery, and toot around on a surrey-with-the-fringe-on-top bike.

Yes, it's heavily themed and that's the idea. But the alcohol and fun are very real. (www.disneyworld.com; 1620 East Buena Vista Dr, Disney Springs; ⏱11:30am-midnight; 🖥Disney, 🚗Disney, 🚌Lynx 50)

Belle Vue Room BAR

22 MAP P40, D5

On the 2nd floor of **Disney's BoardWalk Inn** (☎407-939-5277; www.disneyworld.com; r from $550; 🅿♿❄@🛜🏊), this is an excellent place for a quiet drink. It's more like a sitting room: you can relax and play a board game, listen to classic radio shows such as *Lone Ranger*, or simply take your drink to a rocking chair on the balcony and watch the comings and goings along Disney's BoardWalk. (☎407-939-6200; www.disneyworld.com; 2101 Epcot Resorts Blvd, Disney's BoardWalk Inn; ⏱6:30-11am & 5pm-midnight; 🖥Disney, 🚗Disney)

Entertainment

Drawn to Life PERFORMING ARTS

23 MAP P40, D2

A Disney animator's desk is the stage and the characters are both lithe and alive in this show that debuted in 2020. It combines the visual genius of Walt Disney Imagineering with the mind-boggling acrobatic feats of Cirque du Soleil. This is a small horseshoe theater, with roughly 20 rows from the stage to the top, and no balcony.

Disney built the theater specifically to house the show's predecessor, *La Nouba* – there are no bad seats. See the website for black-out dates. (407-939-7328, 407-939-7600; www.cirquedusoleil. com; 1478 Buena Vista Dr, Disney Springs; adult $67-179, child $65-145; 6pm & 9pm Tue-Sat; Disney, Disney, Lynx 50)

Chip 'n' Dale Campfire Singalong CINEMA

24 MAP P40, C2

This intimate and low-key character experience offers singing and dancing with Chip and Dale, campfires for roasting marshmallows, and a free outdoor screening of a Disney film. Every night is a different movie, and Disney doesn't post a schedule on its website – call or search online.

You can buy generously portioned s'mores supplies, and though there are split-log benches, it's better to bring a blanket and pillows to snuggle down on. Cars are not allowed in Fort Wilderness; park at the parking area after the entry gate, or take a Disney bus or boat to the resort, and catch a shuttle the few minutes to the Meadow Recreation Area. (407-939-7529; www.disneyworld.com; 4510 N Fort Wilderness Trail, Disney's Fort Wilderness Resort; 8pm; Disney, Disney)

Shopping

Lego Imagination Center TOYS

25 MAP P40, F1

Life-size Lego creations, tables to create your own masterpieces and a wall of individually priced Lego pieces. (407-828-0065; www.disneyworld.com; 1672 Buena Vista Dr, Disney Springs; 9am-11pm; Disney, Disney, Lynx 50)

Once Upon a Toy TOYS

26 MAP P40, F1

Design a personalized My Little Pony, build your own lightsaber and create your own tiara at one of the best toy stores anywhere. You'll find old-school classics such as Mr Potato Head and Lincoln Logs, board games, action figures, stuffed animals and more. (407-824-4321; www.disneyworld.com; 1375 Buena Vista Dr, Disney Springs; 10am-11:30pm; Disney, Disney, Lynx 50)

World of Disney GIFTS & SOUVENIRS

27 MAP P40, F1

Room after room of Disney everything at this Disney mega-super-duper store (the country's largest). (407-939-6224; www.disneyworld. com; Disney Springs; 9am-11pm; Disney, Disney, Lynx 50)

Explore ✦
Magic Kingdom

When most people think of Walt Disney World®, they're thinking of just one of the four theme parks – Magic Kingdom. The home of Cinderella Castle, Splash Mountain and many a dream come true isn't just quintessential Disney, but the template for all theme park development and a pilgrimage to the origin of a million childhood fantasies.

The Short List

○ **Disney Enchantment (p52)** *A magical, light-and-fireworks finale to a day in the park.*

○ **Festival of Fantasy (p65)** *Colorful parade starring characters from some of Disney's best-loved films.*

○ **Be Our Guest (p62)** *Fine gourmet dining in the Beast's castle from Beauty and the Beast – and he will make an appearance.*

○ **Fantasyland (p57)** *The heart of Magic Kingdom and a dream come true, especially for the under-eights.*

○ **Splash Mountain (p61)** *Thrilling coaster with a 40mph drop into water that will leave you wet and screaming with joy.*

Getting There & Around

🚌 From Disney hotels or the Transportation & Ticket Center (TTC).

🚝 From Disney's Contemporary, Grand Floridian or Polynesian Village resorts.

⛴ From Disney's Fort Wilderness Resort, Disney's Wilderness Lodge and TTC.

🚗 Park at the TTC.

Region Map on p56

Fantasyland (p57) ROBERTO MACHADO NOA/LIGHTROCKET VIA GETTY IMAGES ©

Top Experience 📷
Watch Fireworks Explode at Disney Enchantment

The grand finale to many a visitor's day in Magic Kingdom is the simply spectacular fireworks-and-light show that lights up the sky above Cinderella Castle. Images of favorite Disney characters, including Moana and Raya, are projected onto the castle walls, with the magically immersive effects extending down Main Street, USA.

◉ MAP P56, D2

www.disneyworld.com

Magic Kingdom

theme-park admission required

🕐 8pm, hours vary

🚌 Disney, 🚢 Disney, 🚌 Lynx 50, 56

Best Viewing Spots

The most magical spot to view the show is on Central Plaza at the top of Main Street, USA, directly in front of the castle. Stand with your back against the fenced-off grassy area surrounding the statue of Walt and Mickey, which is slightly elevated. Alternatively, the eastern side (to the right, if facing the castle) of the plaza is good as it gives you the best view of the show's lovely finale.

There is no FastPass+ arrangement for the show, but book a table or a standing spot at the Tomorrowland Terrace (p64) for its Fireworks Dessert Party and you'll be guaranteed a good view, as you will be with a reservation at the California Grill (p44) in Disney's Contemporary Resort.

The Show

Debuting in October 2021 as part of the Walt Disney World® 50th Anniversary Celebration, this 15-minute spectacular is an invitation to celebrate magic, imagination and personal dreams. Set sail across the sea with Moana, soar above the clouds on Aladdin's magic carpet and join brothers Ian and Barley from Disney and Pixar's *Onward*. In one moving segment, Joe Gardner from the animated film *Soul* takes viewers into 'the zone' to discover a whimsical world inspired by the style of legendary Disney artist Mary Blair.

The projections, lights and fireworks are accompanied by a stirring Disney soundtrack that includes a new song written specifically for the show – 'You Are the Magic' – by Grammy-award-winning songwriter Philip Lawrence. The adventure builds to a crescendo when Tinker Bell takes flight from the castle, scattering pixie dust as she goes (a much-loved event happily repurposed from the previous fireworks incarnation, Happily Ever After).

★ Top Tips

o Show up at least an hour before the show to nab a good spot along Main Street.

o Diners at the rooftop California Grill can eat pre-fireworks and then come back, flash their receipt and re-enter the restaurant for the show.

✖ Take a Break

Load up on ice-cream sandwiches and fresh-baked cookies – the perfect fuel for the fireworks – at Sleepy Hollow (p64).

★ Expensive Dreams

Disney magic takes money and effort: the show costs $25,000 a night to put together and Disney is the second-biggest user of explosives in the US after the Department of Defence.

Walking Tour 🥾

A Classic Day in Magic Kingdom

Magic Kingdom, the oldest theme park at Walt Disney World® Resort, is a must for anyone looking for the nostalgic charm of vintage Disney movies, rides and characters. For this Classic Disney Day, you'll need admission to Magic Kingdom, and, if you can, FastPass+ reservations for Space Mountain and Splash Mountain.

Walk Facts

Start Disney's Contemporary Resort

End Main Street, USA

Length 2 miles; 12 hours

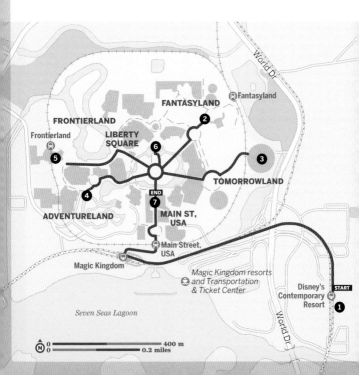

❶ Chef Mickey's

Hugs from Mickey Mouse (and Minnie Mouse, Pluto, Donald Duck and Goofy) first thing in the morning? Yes, please! Reserve well in advance to enjoy an early buffet breakfast (and perhaps a 'Magical Morning Cocktail' or two) at Chef Mickey's (p47), then hop on the monorail and get to Magic Kingdom when the gates open.

❷ Fantasyland

While it's tempting to meander down Main Street, admiring the windows and picking up souvenirs, lines at Disney old-school classics soon stretch beyond an hour so you'll want to get to them first thing. Head to Fantasyland, just beyond the castle, and ride Peter Pan's Flight (p57), the Many Adventures of Winnie-the-Pooh (p58) and the Mad Tea Party (p60), in that order. Then, if you're ready for the earworm, take a gentle boat ride around the globe on it's a small world (p57).

❸ Space Mountain

Scurry over to Tomorrowland for Space Mountain (p61), an outer-space-themed indoor roller coaster that first opened in 1975. The premise here is that you are riding a spaceship through the stratosphere, and the entire ride takes place in darkness with only twinkling stars and zooming galaxies as light.

❹ Jungle Cruise

Some of Magic Kingdom's earliest attractions feel strikingly bizarre and kitsch by today's standards, and that's their charm. You've already encountered singing-and-dancing animatronic children in it's a small world, so now embark on a slow-moving ride past animatronic elephants on the Jungle Cruise (p59) in Adventureland.

❺ Splash Mountain

Hop on a boat (p61) and ride through the 1946 film *Song of the South*, past animatronic Br'er Fox and Br'er Bear, around through the darkness and up, up, up...until you splash down into the water. Be aware you will get *very* wet.

❻ Cinderella's Royal Table

If you've little ones, reserve ahead to dine with a princess at Cinderella's Royal Table (p63), or go the whole Bibbidi Bobbidi Boutique (p65) transformation with a fairy godmother in charge.

❼ Main Street, USA

Magic Kingdom offers concerts (on the steps of Cinderella Castle) and parades throughout the day, with visitors lining up along Main Street, USA (p61), to cheer on the floats. Check the schedule as you come in, and return to the park in the evening for the Disney Enchantment show (p52).

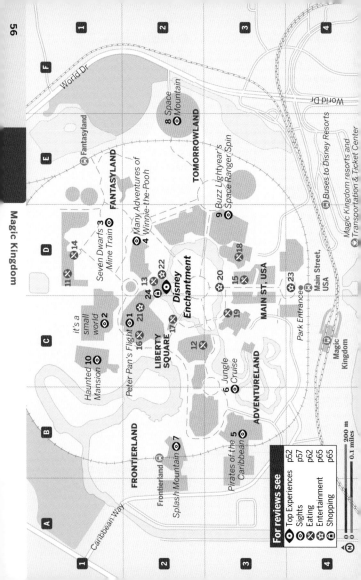

World Dr

Caribbean Way

FRONTIERLAND

Frontierland

Splash Mountain 7

Pirates of the 5
Caribbean

Haunted 10
Mansion

it's a
small
world 2

Peter Pan's Flight 1

16 21

Seven Dwarfs 3
Mine Train

11 14

FANTASYLAND

Fantasyland

8 Space
Mountain

Many Adventures of 4
Winnie-the-Pooh

24 13 22

Disney
Enchantment

17 12

LIBERTY SQUARE

Jungle 6
Cruise

ADVENTURELAND

20 18

15 19

9 Buzz Lightyear's
Space Ranger Spin

TOMORROWLAND

23

Park Entrance

MAIN ST, USA

Main Street,
USA

Magic
Kingdom

World Dr

Magic Kingdom resorts and
Transportation & Ticket Center

Buses to Disney Resorts

For reviews see	
Top Experiences	p52
Sights	p57
Eating	p62
Entertainment	p65
Shopping	p65

200 m
0.1 miles

Sights

Peter Pan's Flight FANTASYLAND

1 ⊙ MAP P56, C2

A Fantasyland classic, this indoor ride starts in the Darling family's house before taking you on an easygoing flight aboard a pirate ship that makes its way through the fog and stars over London before arriving in Neverland. All things end well as Peter saves Wendy and Captain Hook dances on the snout of a crocodile. It's very popular, so use a FastPass+ or get here early to avoid long lines. (www.disneyworld.com; Magic Kingdom, Fantasyland; theme-park admission required; ⊙9am-9pm, hours vary; 🚇Disney, ⛴Disney, 🚌Lynx 50, 56)

it's a small world FANTASYLAND

2 ⊙ MAP P56, C1

Fantasyland's most enduring ride is this sweet boat trip around the globe, which has captivated children since it debuted at the 1964 New York World's Fair. Small boats gently glide through country after country, each decked out from floor to ceiling with elaborate and charmingly dated sets inhabited by hundreds of automated animals and children. Yes, it's so well known how the song sticks irritatingly in your head for weeks, that it's become a Disney cliché. (www.disneyworld.com; Magic Kingdom, Fantasyland; theme-park admission required; ⊙9am-9pm, hours vary; 🚇Disney, ⛴Disney, 🚌Lynx 50, 56)

Magic Kingdom Sights

Big Thunder Mountain Railroad (p60)

Seven Dwarfs Mine Train
FANTASYLAND

3 ⊙ MAP P56, D1

Race and 'heigh-ho' your way through a diamond mine in this family roller coaster that is a Fantasyland favorite. The audio-animatronics are great, but it's the singing that's really infectious. (www.disneyworld.com; Magic Kingdom, Fantasyland; theme-park admission required; ⊙9am-9pm, hours vary; 🚌Disney, ⛴Disney, 🚌Lynx 50, 56)

Many Adventures of Winnie-the-Pooh
FANTASYLAND

4 ⊙ MAP P56, D2

Take a sweet journey through the Hundred Acre Wood aboard a 'Hunny Pot' as Winnie and the gang wish you a 'Happy Winds-day.' A nice dream sequence with Heffalumps and Woozles ends in a satisfying cloudburst. One of Fantasyland's better-done rides. (www.disneyworld.com; Magic Kingdom, Fantasyland; theme-park admission

Discovering the Magic Kingdom Lands

Fantasyland Spread out like a miniature Alpine village under the towers of Cinderella Castle, Fantasyland is the spellbinding heart of the Magic Kingdom, especially for the eight-and-under crowd and grown-ups looking for a nostalgic taste of classic Disney. Littlies, especially, love the character-focused experiences and attractions.

Adventureland Adventure Disney-style means pirates and jungles, magic carpets and tree houses, and whimsical and silly representations of the exotic locales from storybooks and imagination.

Frontierland The theme at this land is 19th-century America, and as you walk through it you may notice a historical timeline, beginning with the establishment of the frontier in the early 1800s to the period just before the Civil War.

Tomorrowland Although the Jetsons-inspired peek into the future falls flat, Tomorrowland holds a couple of wildly popular Disney highlights. At the interactive comedy show *Monsters, Inc Laugh Floor,* monsters from the film must harness human laughter rather than screams. A screen projects characters from the movie, each doing a stand-up comedy routine that surprises audience members by unexpectedly incorporating them. It's pretty funny, and every show is different.

Liberty Square Disney does the birth of America, complete with Federalist architecture.

Jungle Cruise

required; ⊘9am-9pm, hours vary; 🚃Disney, 🚤Disney, 🚃Lynx 50, 56)

Pirates of the Caribbean
ADVENTURELAND

5 ⊙ MAP P56, B3

The ride that spawned the hugely successful movie series remains one of Disney's most popular attractions. Drunken pirates sing pirate songs, sleep among the pigs and sneer over their empty whiskey bottles, but unless you're scared of the dark or growling pirates, it's a giggle not a scream. It's busy, but the lines generally move pretty quickly. Ride in the late afternoon for minimum waiting times. (www.disneyworld.com; Magic Kingdom, Adventureland; theme-park admission required; ⊘9am-9pm, hours vary; 🚃Disney, 🚤Disney, 🚃Lynx 50, 56)

Jungle Cruise
ADVENTURELAND

6 ⊙ MAP P56, B3

This boat ride through a bunch of simulated jungle waterways populated by animatronic animals and people is quite fun, if you can stomach the skipper's cheeseball humor. Bad word play, silly jokes... they're all part of the experience. (www.disneyworld.com; Magic Kingdom, Adventureland; theme-park admission required; ⊘9am-9pm, hours vary; 🚃Disney, 🚤Disney, 🚃Lynx 50, 56)

Other Magic Kingdom Rides & Experiences

Fantasyland

Ride through the *Little Mermaid* on **Under the Sea: Journey of the Little Mermaid**. At **Dumbo the Flying Elephant** toddlers love jumping on a Dumbo and riding slowly around and around, up and down, and thrill at the chance to control how high they go. Lines here can be unbelievably long and slow, and the ride is incredibly short – hit this when the park gates open. The **Mad Tea Party** is a basic spinning ride, and you and others in the teacup decide just how much you'll be twirling.

Adventureland

Kids love flying around on **Magic Carpets of Aladdin**, but skip the slow train of folks climbing 116 steps at **Swiss Family Treehouse**, a replica tree house of the shipwrecked family from the book and movie *The Swiss Family Robinson*. Animatronic birds sing and dance Hawaiian-style at **Walt Disney's Enchanted Tiki Room**, a silly and rather bizarre two-bit attraction that opened in 1963 and continues to enjoy a curious cult following. You won't find lines, and it makes for a perfect spot to relax out of the heat for a bit.

Frontierland

With no steep drops or loop-dee-loops, mild **Big Thunder Mountain Railroad** is a great choice for little ones – and a Disney classic.

Tomorrowland

Kids can put the pedal to the metal on grand-prix-style cars at **Indy Speedway**, but the cars are fixed to the track and you don't control the steering. Note that kids must be 52in tall to 'drive' on their own.

Liberty Square

The **Hall of Presidents** is a superpatriotic flick on US history. More fun is the regular **Muppets Present...Great Moments in American History** show, a zany eight-minute trip through US history that takes place throughout the day on the square.

You can take to the water aboard the **Liberty Belle Riverboat**, which departs every half hour and goes for a 15-minute cruise around Tom Sawyer Island.

Splash Mountain   FRONTIERLAND

7 ◉ MAP P56, B2

Wild West Disney-style Splash Mountain (FastPass+) depicts the misadventures of Br'er Rabbit, Br'er Bear and Br'er Fox, complete with chatty frogs, singing ducks and other critters. The ride is half a mile long and the 40mph drop into the river makes for one of the biggest thrills in the park – and you will get very wet! The best ride in Frontierland and a highlight of any visit to Walt Disney World®. (www.disneyworld.com; Magic Kingdom, Frontierland; theme-park admission required; ⏱9am-9pm, hours vary; 🚌Disney, 🚢Disney, 🚌Lynx 50, 56)

Space Mountain   TOMORROWLAND

8 ◉ MAP P56, E2

The Magic Kingdom's most popular ride is this indoor coaster that rockets its way through the star-studded galaxies of outer space. It's fast (in Disney terms at least) and while there are no long drops, the sudden turns and near darkness are what give this classic coaster its thrills. It's in Tomorrowland's most futuristic-looking structure. Come first thing or use FastPass+. (www.disneyworld.com; Magic Kingdom, Tomorrowland; theme-park admission required; ⏱9am-9pm, hours vary; 🚌Disney, 🚢Disney, 🚌Lynx 50, 56)

Strolling Main Street, USA

All visits to the Magic Kingdom begin and end on Main Street, which was fashioned after Walt Disney's hometown of Marceline, MO, but given the full Disney treatment. Built to four-fifths scale, the Victorian-style, pastel-colored buildings are power-hosed every night and repainted regularly, all to cast that spell that is at the heart of Disney's own brand of magic.

At the top of the street is **Central Plaza**, which is the main gathering point for the crowds who congregate for the nightly fireworks-and-light shows. There are no big-ticket attractions, but you can meet Mickey Mouse, and Tinker Bell and her friends from Pixie Hollow at the **Town Square Theater Meet and Greets** (FastPass+); peruse the miniature dioramas of Peter Pan and Snow White in the street windows; pop in to catch the black-and-white movie reels of old Disney cartoons; and browse the thousands of must-have Disney souvenirs.

The only ride – Walt Disney World® Railroad – is closed pending the construction of a new *Tron*-themed ride in nearby Tomorrowland.

Magical Character Encounters

Fantasyland offers all kinds of excellent character-interaction opportunities. Spend time with Merida in the little stone grotto of **Fairytale Garden**; listen to Belle tell a story at **Enchanted Tales with Belle**; meet Ariel at **Ariel's Grotto** and Gaston by **Gaston's Tavern**; or hop in line and catch a handful of princesses in **Fairytale Hall**. And, of course, always keep an eye out for Alice in Wonderland, Cinderella and other favorites hanging out throughout.

Note: Mary Poppins is, er, a 'floater'; she appears at different lands at different times. Ask a staff member (known as a 'cast character') where she might be appearing.

Buzz Lightyear's Space Ranger Spin
TOMORROWLAND

10 ◉ MAP P56, D3

Join Buzz in his efforts to save the world from the evil Emperor Zurg. A cross between a ride and a video game, the aim is to shoot a laser at targets projected onto the screens. It's a tad clunky but brilliant fun. (www.disneyworld.com; Magic Kingdom, Tomorrowland; theme-park admission required; ☺9am-9pm, hours vary; 🚌Disney, 🚌Lynx 50, 56)

Haunted Mansion
LIBERTY SQUARE

10 ◉ MAP P56, C1

Liberty Square's best attraction is this classic favorite, which is a low-on-thrill, high-on-silly bit of fun. Cruise slowly past the haunted dining room, where apparitions dance across the stony floor, but beware of those hitchhiking ghosts – don't be surprised if they jump into your car uninvited. While it's mostly lighthearted ghosty goofiness, kids may be frightened by spooky preride dramatics. (www.disneyworld.cm; Magic Kingdom, Liberty Square; theme-park admission required; ☺9am-9pm, hours vary; 🚌Disney, 🚢Disney, 🚌Lynx 50, 56)

Eating

Be Our Guest
AMERICAN $$$

11 ✖ MAP P56, D1

Set inside the Beast's marvelously detailed castle, this experience is a must for *Beauty and the Beast* fans. With three 'Royal Rooms' for 'loyal subjects', table-service meals are a treat. Specialties in the three-course prix-fixe plan include the French onion soup, the pork tenderloin and the dark chocolate truffle. (📞407-939-3463; www.disneyworld.com; Magic Kingdom; prix-fixe adult/child lunch or dinner $62/37, theme-park admission required; ☺11am-2:30pm & 4-10pm, hours vary; 📶♿; 🚌Disney, 🚢Disney 🚌Lynx 50, 56)

Jungle Navigation Co Ltd Skipper Canteen
INTERNATIONAL $$

2 🍴 MAP P56, C2

This adventure-themed spot has three delightful areas based around boat skippers' tropical headquarters in the days of boat exploration. Enjoy a meal in the Secret Society of Adventurers Room, the Jungle Room or the Mess. It's the most atmospheric of options in the park and the meals are large, but by far the healthiest. The menu features 'sustainable fish' and Skip's Beefy Bakes pasta. (📞407-939-5277; www.disneyworld.com; Magic Kingdom; mains $19-38, theme-park admission required; ⏱11:30am-9pm)

Cinderella's Royal Table
AMERICAN $$$

3 🍴 MAP P56, D2

Cinderella greets guests and sits for a portrait (included in the price), and a sit-down meal with princesses (Aurora, Ariel and Snow White) is served upstairs. The food's good, but it's the sight of those deliriously happy kids in princess costumes that makes it special. This is the only restaurant in the castle – make reservations six months in advance. (📞407-934-7927; www.disneyworld.com; Cinderella Castle, Magic Kingdom; adult/child from $75/45, theme-park admission required; ⏱8-10:15am, 11:30am-2:50pm & 4-10:20pm, hours vary; 🛜 👶; 🚌Disney, 🚤Disney, 🚌Lynx 50, 56)

Gaston's Tavern
AMERICAN $

14 🍴 MAP P56, D1

The manliest of manly Disney characters gets a themed snack bar, where you can get fresh sandwiches and cinnamon rolls. Try Le Fou's Brew, Disney's counter to Universal's runaway hit Butterbeer. (www.disneyworld.com; Magic Kingdom; mains $8-10, theme-park admission required; ⏱9am-park closing; 🛜👶; 🚌Disney, 🚤Disney, 🚌Lynx 50, 56)

Main Street Bakery
BAKERY $

15 🍴 MAP P56, D3

Few places require good strong java more than Walt Disney World®, and few places are as notorious for bad coffee as the Happiest Place on Earth. Main Street Bakery has Starbucks. It might (or might not) be the answer to your prayers. (www.disneyworld.com; Magic Kingdom; items $5-10, theme-park admission required; ⏱9am-park closing; 🚌Disney, 🚤Disney, 🚌Lynx 50, 56)

Columbia Harbour House
AMERICAN $

16 🍴 MAP P56, C2

One of the better counter-service restaurants in the Magic Kingdom is this nautical-themed spot with an interior styled like an old boat. Seafood and fish make up the bulk of the menu (the grilled salmon is lovely), but there's also chicken, mac 'n' cheese and a good tomato-and-hummus sandwich. (www.disneyworld.com; Magic Kingdom; mains $9-16, theme-park admission required; ⊙11am–park closing; 📶♿; 🚌Disney, 🚢Disney, 🚌Lynx 50, 56)

Sleepy Hollow

AMERICAN $

17 🏷 MAP P56, C2

This small walk-up 'window' produces a yummy ice-cream sandwich with oozing vanilla ice cream squished between warm, fresh-baked chocolate-chip cookies. Look for the brick house in Liberty Square, just across the bridge from Cinderella Castle. Ideal snacks for the fireworks. (www.disneyworld.com; Magic Kingdom; snacks $6-9, theme-park admission required; ⊙9am–park closing; 🚌Disney, 🚢Disney, 🚌Lynx 50, 56)

Be Our Guest (p62)

© DISNEY

Tomorrowland Terrace

AMERICAN $

18 🏷 MAP P56, D3

Burgers make up the main fare at this casual spot, but in the evening it's all about the Fireworks Dessert Party (adult/child $114/69), where diners are fed an assortment of sweet treats while enjoying a great view of the fireworks behind Cinderella Castle. There's also a standing version, in a closed-off area of Plaza Garden (adult/child $99/59). (www.disneyworld.com; Magic Kingdom, Tomorrowland; mains $11-13, theme-park admission required ⊙9am-9pm, hours vary; 🚌Disney, 🚌Lynx 50, 56)

Crystal Palace

AMERICAN $$$

19 🏷 MAP P56, C3

The buffet at this character meal inside Magic Kingdom is surprisingly tasty. At lunch, there's a wide selection of salads, glazed carrots, mashed potatoes and green beans, as well as a carving station with ham and steak. The real draw, though, is the glass-enclosed garden atmosphere and Winnie-the-Pooh and friends mingling around the tables. (📞407-939-3463; www.disneyworld.com; Magic Kingdom; buffet adult/child $39/23, theme-park admission required; ⊙8-10:45am, 11:30am-2:45pm & 3:15-9:15pm, hours vary; 🚌Disney, 🚢Disney, 🚌Lynx 50, 56)

Entertainment

Festival of Fantasy PARADE

10 ⭐ MAP P56, D3

The vivid pageantry of Fantasyland and its colorful cast of characters are part of this parade that makes its way down Main Street, USA. Characters from *Frozen, The Little Mermaid* and *Brave* feature, as do Rapunzel, Peter Pan and Sleeping Beauty. Plus Maleficent, the fire-breathing dragon. (www.disneyworld.com; Magic Kingdom; theme-park admission required; ⏰morning & afternoon daily, hours vary; 🚌Disney, 🚢Disney, 🚌Lynx 50, 56)

Mickey's PhilharMagic CINEMA

11 ⭐ MAP P56, C2

Undoubtedly the best 3D show in Disney, Mickey's PhilharMagic takes Donald Duck on a whimsical adventure through classic Disney movies. Ride with him through the streets of Morocco on Aladdin's carpet and feel the champagne on your face when it pops open during *Beauty and the Beast's* 'Be Our Guest.' Fun, silly and lighthearted, this is Disney at its best. (www.disneyworld.com; Magic Kingdom, Fantasyland; theme-park admission required; ⏰9am-9pm, hours vary; 🚌Disney, 🚌Lynx 50, 56)

Once Upon a Time LIGHT SHOW

12 ⭐ MAP P56, D2

Seasonally changing light-and-music show that's projected onto Cinderella Castle. It highlights Disney movies and characters, and takes place before or after Disney Enchantment (aka the 'Nighttime Spectacular'). (www.disneyworld.com; Magic Kingdom; theme-park admission required; ⏰nightly, hours vary; 🚌Disney, 🚢Disney, 🚌Lynx 50, 56)

Mickey's Not-So-Scary Halloween Party CARNIVAL

23 ⭐ MAP P56, D4

Characters decked out in costumes, trick-or-treating, a Halloween-inspired parade, and fireworks and events. Discounted tickets available if purchased in advance online. (📞407-939-5277; www.disneyworld.com; Magic Kingdom; adult/child from $109/99, theme-park entry from 4pm included in ticket price; ⏰select nights Sep & Oct; 🚌Disney, 🚢Disney, 🚌Lynx 50, 56)

Shopping

Bibbidi Bobbidi Boutique COSMETICS

24 🔒 MAP P56, D2

Inside Cinderella Castle, fairy godmothers finalize your kid's transformation from shorts and T-shirt to bedazzling princess with hairstyling and makeup, or knight with outfit, sword and shield.

There's a second Bibbidi Bobbidi in Disney Springs. (📞407-939-7895; www.disneyworld.com; Magic Kingdom; hair & makeup from $79; ⏰10am-8pm, hours vary)

Explore ⊘

Disney's Hollywood Studios

Hollywood's Golden Age may be the thematic inspiration for Disney's Hollywood Studios, but once you move beyond the art deco entrance and the versions of 1930s Tinseltown, this park is all about today's star power. There's Pixar, Frozen and other attractions, but they've all been overshadowed by the brightest star of all – Star Wars: Galaxy's Edge.

The Short List

○ **Star Wars: Galaxy's Edge (p68)** *Travel to a galaxy far, far away and immerse yourself in the Star Wars universe.*

○ **Star Wars: Rise of the Resistance (p69)** *Less a ride and more of a high-tech, immersive experience.*

○ **Rock 'n' Roller Coaster Starring Aerosmith (p71)** *Take off at high speed and do a couple of inversions at a g-force of 5.*

○ **50's Prime Time Café (p72)** *Home-cooked meals in a restaurant designed to look like a suburban house from the 1950s.*

○ **Twilight Zone Tower of Terror (p71)** *Ride the elevator of terror and get ready for some hidden surprises!*

Getting There & Around

🚌 From Disney hotels or the Transportation & Ticket Center.

⛴ From Disney's Hollywood Studios, Epcot (and its resorts) and Disney's BoardWalk.

Region Map on p70

Twilight Zone Tower of Terror (p71) © DISNEY

Top Experience 📷

Explore the Galaxy's Edge with Star Wars

The transformation of a 14-acre backlot into the Black Spire Outpost, a spaceport on remote Batuu, is Disney's most ambitious technological accomplishment to date. Every detail is remarkable, from the buildings to the full-scale Millennium Falcon and the live actor performances. The two rides are exceptional and the land is a new standard in immersive theme park design.

◎ MAP P70, A6

www.disneyworld.com

Hollywood Studios

theme-park admission required

🕐 9am-9pm, hours vary

🚌 Disney, 🚢 Disney

Millennium Falcon: Smuggler's Run

Climb aboard the mythical Millennium Falcon and your crew of six – two pilots, two gunners and two engineers – try to fly the 'fastest hunk of junk in the galaxy' on a less-than-legit mission. The special effects (including jumping to light speed) are very good, but this is effectively an immersive video game where you just press a lot of buttons, which may disappoint some. However, the thrill of being aboard a full-scale version of Han and Chewy's ship might suffice.

Star Wars: Rise of the Resistance

Rise of the Resistance isn't so much a ride as a 20-minute-long, multi-part piece of high-tech theater that seamlessly blends four ride systems and a stunning walkthrough experience that drew gasps of delighted wonder when we visited. The plot is straightforward: you're a crew member on a transport that is captured by the First Order and, after being tractor-beamed into the belly of an Imperial Star Destroyer, your task is to escape.

Galaxy's Edge Retail

The souk-style marketplace sells all kinds of merch. At **Savi's Workshop** you can design your own lightsaber; at **Mubo's Droid Depot** you can build a BB or R-series droid; while at **Bina's Creature Stall** you can adopt a little baby Rathtar among other galactic animals.

Virtual Lines

In order to deal with the massive numbers looking to get on Star Wars: Rise of the Resistance, Disney instituted a virtual line system, which is available through the My Disney Experience app, but only works once you're in the park. You join a boarding group and then receive a time slot for joining the ride. Until the hype dies down, you won't be able to use FastPass+ to gain entry.

★ Top Tips

○ The more accurate you are during Millennium Falcon: Smuggler's Run, the longer the ride lasts.

○ The Play Disney Parks app lets you personalize your *Star Wars* adventure by immersing you more fully into Galaxy's Edge: take a side, perform tasks, embark on a mission...

○ Galaxy's Edge's live actors will always stay in character, so stormtroopers will bark at you to move, Kylo Ren is *always* surly and Chewbacca is friendly but mistrustful.

✕ Take a Break

Grab a drink among the bounty hunters, smugglers and rogues that frequent **Oga's Cantina** (pictured; www.disneyworld.com; Disney's Hollywood Studios, Star Wars: Galaxy's Edge; alcoholic drinks $16-19, non-alcoholic drinks $7-13, theme-park admission required; ⊙9am-9pm, hours vary).

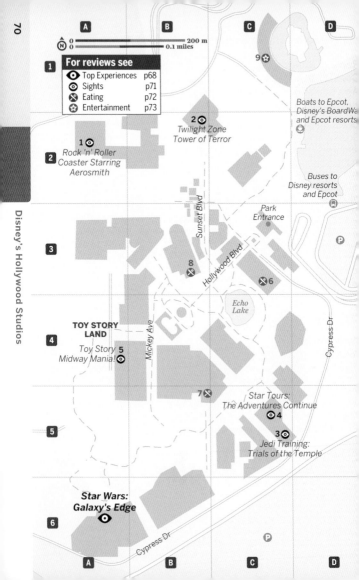

N
0 ——————————— 200 m
0 ——————————— 0.1 miles

For reviews see
◉ Top Experiences   p68
◉ Sights   p71
✕ Eating   p72
☆ Entertainment   p73

1 ◉ Rock 'n' Roller Coaster Starring Aerosmith

2 ◉ Twilight Zone Tower of Terror

9 ☆

Boats to Epcot, Disney's BoardWa and Epcot resorts

Buses to Disney resorts and Epcot

Park Entrance

Sunset Blvd

Hollywood Blvd

8 ✕

✕ 6

Echo Lake

P

TOY STORY LAND

Toy Story 5 Midway Mania! ◉

Mickey Ave

7 ✕

Star Tours: The Adventures Continue
◉ 4

3 ◉ Jedi Training: Trials of the Temple

Cypress Dr

Star Wars: Galaxy's Edge ◉

Cypress Dr

P

Sights

Rock 'n' Roller Coaster Starring Aerosmith
SUNSET BOULEVARD

⊙ MAP P70, A2

One of the best indoor coasters in Orlando, where you take off up a ramp, going from 0mph to 57mph in three seconds before twisting into an inversion at a g-force of 5. A bunch of loops and twists later and you've arrived – all to a raucous Aerosmith soundtrack. Not for the fainthearted: the speed and twists are one thing, but doing them in semi-darkness will put others off. Not us, though. Can we go again? It's at the top of Sunset Boulevard. www.disneyworld.com; Disney's Hollywood Studios; theme-park admission required; ⊙9am-9pm, hours vary; Disney, Disney)

Twilight Zone Tower of Terror
SUNSET BOULEVARD

⊙ MAP P70, B2

On your tour of this now decrepit Hollywood hotel, the elevator taking you to the 13th floor experiences a series of strange events, including sudden drops and lifts and then... OK, we don't want to give anything away, but this is a brilliantly executed ride, full of minutely observed detail. From the top, you can get a (quick) glimpse of the whole park. www.disneyworld.com; theme-park admission required; ⊙9am-9pm, hours vary; Disney, Disney)

Jedi Training: Trials of the Temple
ECHO LAKE

3 ⊙ MAP P70, C5

Children aged four to 12, don brown robes, pledge the sacred Jedi oath and grab a lightsaber for on-stage training by a Jedi Master. The Force is invoked a number of times, and trainees receive a diploma for their participation. It's first-come, first-served, so get to Disney's Hollywood Studios when gates open and line up at the Indiana Adventure Outpost, near the 50's Prime Time Café, to sign up for one of the many daily classes. (www.disneyworld.com; Disney's Hollywood Studios; theme-park admission required; ⊙from 9am, up to 15 times daily)

50's Prime Time Café (p72)

Disney's Hollywood Studios Sights

Lands of Disney's Hollywood Studios ⓘ

Sunset Boulevard The heart of the original park evokes the glamour of 1940s Hollywood. There are lots of eating options, as well as some of the park's better rides.

Hollywood Boulevard & Echo Lake This is where you'll find the *Star Wars*–themed Star Tours (FastPass+), one of Disney's best 3D-simulated experiences, the over-the-top stunt show **Indiana Jones Epic Stunt Spectacular** (FastPass+), held in a huge outdoor theater, and Frozen's **For the First Time in Forever Sing-Along**.

Toy Story Land Everything is oversized in this 11-acre land – but that's because you've been shrunk to the size of a toy and are now in Andy's backyard, where you can play with all the other toys from the *Toy Story* universe. **Alien Swirling Saucers** is a pleasant teacup ride, while **Slinky Dog Dash** is a family-friendly roller coaster. This is a lovely part of the park, especially for younger kids.

Star Tours: The Adventures Continue
ECHO LAKE

4 ◉ MAP P70, C5

Board a *StarSpeeder 1000* and blast into the galaxy at this 3D *Star Wars*–themed simulation ride. (www.disneyworld.com; Disney's Hollywood Studios; theme-park admission required; ◷9am-9pm, hours vary; 🚹; 🚌Disney, 🚢Disney)

Toy Story Midway Mania!
TOY STORY LAND

5 ◉ MAP P70, A4

Don your 3D glasses and you'll be transported inside Andy's toy box, where from inside your car you shoot at all kinds of carnival targets to rack up points. (www.disneyworld.com; Disney's Hollywood Studios; theme-park admission required; ◷9am-9pm, hours vary; 🚌Disney, 🚢Disney)

Eating

50's Prime Time Café
AMERICAN $$

6 ✖ MAP P70, C3

Step into a quintessential 1950s home with TVs, linoleum floors, some of the funkiest of funky retro furniture around and, of course, home-cooked meals, including Grandpa Jean's Chicken Pot Pie, Aunt Liz's Golden Fried Chicken and Mom's Old-Fashioned Pot Roast, served up on a Formica tabletop.

Waiters in pink plaid and white aprons banter playfully and admonish those diners who don't finish their meals with a sassy 'shame, shame, shame.' Such, such fun. (📞407-939-3463; www. disneyworld.com; Disney's Holly-wood Studios; mains $17-27, theme-park admission required; ⏰11am-park closing; 📶👫; 🚊Disney, 🚤Disney)

Sci-Fi
Dine-In Theater   AMERICAN $$

7 ❌ MAP P70, B5

Burgers, ribs and glow-in-the-dark drinks served drive-in style. Climb into your convertible Cadillac, order from the car hop, sip on a Lunar Landing and sit back for animations, a silly horror movie or sci-fi flick (on loop for 47 minutes). There's a handful of normal tables on the side, but if you want your table in a car, request one up to six months in advance. (📞407-939-3463; www.disneyworld.com; Disney's Hollywood Studios; mains $17-33, theme-park admission required; ⏰11am-8:30pm; 📶👫; 🚊Disney, 🚤Disney)

Hollywood
Brown Derby   AMERICAN $$$

8 ❌ MAP P70, B3

Semi-upscale surroundings modeled after the LA original, with an odd selection of gourmet eats ranging from a vegetarian pho (noodle soup) to charred fillet of beef and, of course, that Derby classic, the Cobb salad. This is heavy fare, not the place for a quick light lunch. (📞407-939-3463; www.disneyworld.com; Disney's Hollywood Studios; mains $19-49, theme-park admission required; ⏰11:30am-park closing; 📶👫; 🚊Disney, 🚤Disney)

Entertainment

Fantasmic   LIGHT SHOW

9 ⭐ P70, C1

This water, music and light show features Mickey Mouse as the Sorcerer's Apprentice from *Fantasia*, and involves him using all kinds of wizardry to defeat a cast of Disney villains. The plot's a bit weak but no matter: the effects are spectacular, and get a lot of oohs and aahs from the huge crowd.

Seating for the 25-minute show begins 90 minutes in advance, and even though the outdoor amphitheater seats more than 6000 people, it's always crowded. (📞407-939-5277; www.disneyworld. com; Disney's Hollywood Studios; theme-park admission required; ⏰nightly; 👫; 🚊Disney, 🚤Disney)

Explore

Epcot

Epcot – an acronym of Experimental Prototype Community of Tomorrow – is in the middle of an extensive refurb, with major new rides and experiences being added. Most of the work is taking place in Future World, but the park's other great attraction, World Showcase, is still very much open for business.

The Short List

- ***World Showcase (p77)*** *Explore the cuisines and cultures of 11 countries around the world, conveniently positioned around the same lagoon.*
- ***Frozen Ever After (p78)*** *Travel to Elsa's ice palace aboard a dragon-headed boat while singing songs from Frozen.*
- ***Soarin' Around the World (p77)*** *Enjoy a simulated bird's-eye trip around the world on this superb ride.*
- ***Monsieur Paul (p79)*** *Exquisite French cuisine courtesy of the culinary expertise of Jérôme Bocuse, son of legendary chef Paul.*
- ***La Cava del Tequila (p81)*** *Fine margaritas and more than 220 types of tequila at this Mexican-style cantina.*

Getting There & Around

Direct line to Transportation & Ticket Center.

Connection to Transportation & Ticket Center and Disney's Hollywood Studios.

To Animal Kingdom, Disney's Hollywood Studios and Disney resorts.

Region Map on p76

Spaceship Earth (p79) © DISNEY

Epcot

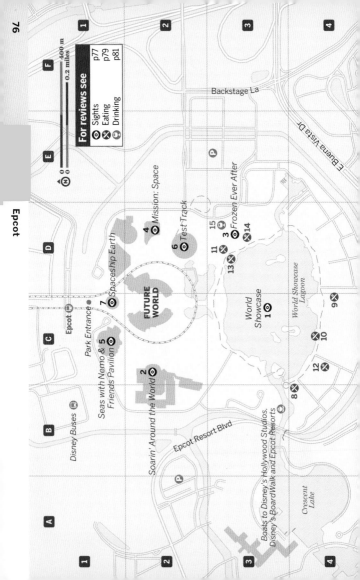

For reviews see
⊙ Sights   p77
⊗ Eating   p79
🍷 Drinking   p81

Backstage La

E Buena Vista Dr

0   400 m
0   0.2 miles

Disney Buses

Epcot
Park Entrance

Seas with Nemo & 5
Friends Pavilion ⊙

Spaceship Earth ⊙

7 ⊙

FUTURE
WORLD

Soarin' Around the World ⊙ 2

Mission: Space ⊙

4

Test Track ⊙

6 ⊙

15
9
3 ⊙ Frozen Ever After
⊗14

11
13 ⊗

World
Showcase ⊙ 1

World Showcase
Lagoon

12 ⊗
8 ⊗

10 ⊗

9 ⊗

Epcot Resort Blvd

Boats to Disney's Hollywood Studios,
Disney's BoardWalk and Epcot Resorts

Crescent Lake

Sights

World Showcase
AREA

1 ⊙ MAP P76, C3

Who needs the hassle of a passport and jet lag when you can travel the world right here at Walt Disney World®? World Showcase, one of two themed sections of Epcot, comprises 11 countries arranged around a lagoon. Watch belly dancing in Morocco, eat pizza in Italy and buy personally engraved bottles of perfume in France, before settling down to watch fireworks about world peace and harmony. Disney was right: it truly is a small world after all.

Seasoned travelers may scoff at the ersatz quality of it all, but so what? The idea here is to prompt you to hop on a plane and explore the real thing; in the meantime, this is a fun way to show kids a little something about the world. The best way to experience the World Showcase is to simply wander as the mood moves you, poking through stores and restaurants, and catching what amounts to Bureau of Tourism promotional films and gentle rides through some of the countries. Highlights include the **American Adventure** in the USA pavilion, a 30-minute dash through US history complete with stirring music, a huge screen and 35 audio-animatronic figures; travelling through Mexico with Donald Duck and his pals in **Gran**

Fiesta Tour Starring the Three Caballeros; and the immensely popular **Frozen Ever After** (p78) boat ride in Norway. The featured countries clockwise around the water are Mexico, Norway, China, Germany, Italy, USA ('The American Adventure'), Japan, Morocco, France, the UK and Canada. (www.disneyworld.com; Epcot; theme-park admission required; ⊙9am-6pm, hours vary; 🚇Disney, 🚢Disney, 🚍Disney)

Soarin' Around the World
RIDE

2 ⊙ MAP P76, C2

Soar up and down, hover and accelerate as the giant screen in front of you takes you over and around the globe. Sounds straightforward, but this is an extraordinarily visceral experience as aroma effects blast the smells of the earth at you as you ride (such as the elephants and grasses of Africa). Ask for a front-row seat; feet dangling in front of you can ruin the effect.

While not at all scary in terms of speed or special effects, people with agoraphobia or motion sickness may feel a bit uneasy. Reserve a FastPass+ or hit this first thing in the morning, as it's one of the best rides at Disney. (www.disneyworld.com; Future World, Epcot; theme-park admission required; ⊙9am-6pm, hours vary; 🚇Disney, 🚢Disney, 🚍Disney)

Test Track

Frozen Ever After
RIDE

3 ⊙ MAP P76, D3

The hottest ride in the World Showcase is this *Frozen*-themed slow boat journey aboard a dragon-headed longboat through the film's familiar settings. There's all of your favorite tunes and some of the film's best-loved characters, brilliantly rendered in animatronic form. The journey ends, inevitably, at Elsa's ice palace. The cold definitely won't bother you. (www.disneyworld.com; Norway, Epcot; ⊘9am-6pm, hours vary)

Mission: Space
RIDE

4 ⊙ MAP P76, D2

The year is 2036 and you're a test pilot at the International Space Training Center. You're assigned a seat in the four-person launch capsule and then it's liftoff. This is an intense simulator ride designed to replicate the g-force of takeoff and a moment of zero-gravity weightlessness. The ride's intensity may cause motion sickness, so choose orange to be on the spinning version of the ride or green on the non-spinning team. (www.disneyworld.com; Future World, Epcot; theme-park admission required; ⊘9am-6pm, hours vary; ⊟Disney, ⊠Disney, ⊟Disney)

Seas with Nemo & Friends Pavilion
RIDE

5 ⊙ MAP P76, C1

Kids under 10 won't want to miss the two *Nemo*-themed attractions at Epcot's Future World. Ride a clamshell through the ocean with

Nemo on **Seas with Nemo & Friends** and talk face-to-face with Crush in the interactive **Turtle Talk with Crush**, a Disney highlight.

A small blue room with a large movie screen holds about 10 rows of benches with sitting room for kids in front. Crush talks to the children staring up at him, taking questions from the 'dude in the dark-blue shell' and cracking jokes about how sea grass gives him the bubbles. Dory shows up and gets squished against the screen by the whale, and there's plenty of silliness and giggling. (www.disneyworld.com; Future World, Epcot; theme-park admission required; 9am-6pm, hours vary; Disney, Disney, Disney)

Test Track
RIDE

6 MAP P76, D2

Board a car and ride through heat, cold, speed, braking and crash tests. At one point a huge semi with blinding lights heads right for you, its horn blaring. When testing the acceleration, the car speeds up to 60mph within a very short distance, but there are few turns and no ups and downs like a roller coaster.

At the ride's entrance you can virtually design your own car, and at the exit you'll find all kinds of car-themed games and simulators. (www.disneyworld.com; Future World, Epcot; theme-park admission required; 9am-6pm, hours vary; Disney, Disney, Disney)

Spaceship Earth
RIDE

7 MAP P76, C1

Epcot's iconic dome is home to this cult favorite ride that explores human progress and the development of communications. From cave paintings to computers, the history of human progress is tracked in slow-moving, kitschy, out-of-date animatronic detail. It's Western-centric, completely devoid of excitement and yet...there's always a line to get on.

At the time of writing there were vague plans to update this ride completely. (www.disneyworld.com; Future World, Epcot; theme-park admission required; 9am-6pm, hours vary; Disney, Disney, Disney)

Eating

Monsieur Paul
FRENCH $$$

8 MAP P76, B4

This exemplary French restaurant atop the France Pavilion bears the imprint of French culinary royalty. Jérôme Bocuse, son of legendary chef Paul, serves up exquisite dishes that would pass muster even in the most discerning Parisian restaurant. The only reminder that you're in Disney is if you sit by the window looking down on World Showcase. (407-939-3463; www.disneyworld.com; France, Epcot; mains $41-47, prix fixe $175; theme-park admission required; 5:30-9pm; Disney, Disney, Disney)

Tutto Gusto

ITALIAN $$

9 ✗ MAP P76, C4

Full marks for this authentic Italian brasserie and wine bar. It oozes style and serves delicious small plates, including meats and cheeses. Definitely the place to come for an excellent glass of Italian wine and homemade pasta served at the bar, high bar tables or while you're nestled on a sofa. Recommended for dinner before the evening spectaculars at Epcot. (☎407-939-3463; www.disneyworld. com; Italy, Epcot; mains $22-36; ⏱11:30am-9pm; ❄🛜; 🚃Disney, ⛴Disney, 🚝Disney)

Teppan Edo

JAPANESE $$$

10 ✗ MAP P76, C4

Chefs toss the chicken, fling the chopsticks and frenetically slice and dice the veggies in this standard cook-in-front-of-you eatery next to Japan's gardens. It's housed in a stunning Japanese building, decked out in a black-and-red color theme and with contemporary flair. Its sister restaurant, **Tokyo Dining** (mains $21-34), is next door. (☎407-939-3463; www.disneyworld.com; Japan, Epcot; mains $30-46, theme-park admission required; ⏱11am-park closing; 🚻; 🚃Disney, ⛴Disney, 🚝Disney)

La Cantina
de San Angel

MEXICAN $

11 ✗ MAP P76, D3

One of the best fast-food places in the park. Try the tacos, served with surprisingly tasty *pico de gallo* (fresh salsa of tomatoes, onion and jalapeños) and fresh avocado. Great guacamole, too. (www.disney world.com; Mexico, Epcot; mains $12-16, theme-park admission required; ⏱11am-park closing; 🛜🖊; 🚃Disney, ⛴Disney, 🚝Disney)

Restaurant
Marrakesh

MEDITERRANEAN $$

12 ✗ MAP P76, C4

Belly dancers shimmy and shake past the massive pillars and around the tables of the Sultan's Palace, magnificently decorated with mosaic tiles, rich velvets and sparkling gold. While the beef kebabs, vegetable couscous and other basics are OK, the window-less elegance in the **Morocco Pavilion** is a fun escape from the searing sun, and kids love to join in the dancing. (☎407-939-3463; www. disneyworld.com; Morocco, Epcot; mains $22-33, theme-park admission required; ⏱11:30am-park closing; 🛜🖊🚻; 🚃Disney, ⛴Disney, 🚝Disney)

La Hacienda
de San Angel

MEXICAN $$

13 ✗ MAP P76, D3

Authentic Mexican rather than Tex Mex, this lagoonside eatery is tops for location and features excellent specials from chicken to seared-meat specialties. Why not make a day of it with on-the-rocks margaritas, ranging from avocado-infused to a classic with cactus lemongrass salt on the rim? (☎407-939-3463; www.disneyworld.

com; Mexico, Epcot; mains $27-35, theme-park admission required; ⏱4pm–park closing; 🚻; 🚌Disney, 🚤Disney, 🚝Disney)

Akershus Royal Banquet Hall NORWEGIAN $$$

14 ✘ MAP P76, D3

Join Disney princesses (a selection of Snow White, Cinderella, Belle, Aurora or Ariel) for a Norwegian-inspired feast in a medieval castle setting – Disney-style, of course, so you'll find pizza and Minute Maid lemonade with a glowing Ariel alongside Norwegian meatballs with lingonberries. It's one of the better character meals, both in terms of ambience and food. (📞407-939-3463; www.disneyworld. com; Norway, Epcot; buffet adult/child $63/41, theme-park admission required; ⏱8-11am, noon-3:30pm & 5-8:30pm; 🚌Disney, 🚤Disney, 🚝Disney)

Drinking

La Cava del Tequila BAR

15 🍸 MAP P76, D3

Pop in for a cucumber, passion fruit or blood-orange margarita. Can't decide? Try a flight of margaritas or shots. The menu features more than 220 types of tequila, and it's a cozy, dark spot, with tiled floors, Mexican-styled murals and a beamed ceiling. (📞407-939-3463; www.disneyworld.com; Mexico, Epcot; theme-park admission required; ⏱11am–park closing; 🚌Disney, 🚤Disney, 🚝Disney)

Morocco Pavilion

Animal Kingdom

Set apart from the rest of Disney both in miles and in tone, Animal Kingdom blends theme park and zoo, carnival and African safari, with a healthy dose of Disney characters, storytelling and transformative magic, not least in Pandora – The World of Avatar, a whole land designed to replicate in all its wondrous beauty the planet from the popular film.

The Short List

○ **Pandora – The World of Avatar (p84)** *Behold the Valley of Mo'ara, with upside-down islands, brilliantly exotic foliage and two excellent rides.*

○ **Avatar: Flight of Passage (p85)** *Perhaps the best ride of all Disney parks is this virtual journey aboard a banshee, Na'vi-style.*

○ **Finding Nemo: the Musical (p89)** *Superb show with music composed by the authors of Frozen and puppets created by the minds behind The Lion King.*

○ **Africa (p87)** *A recreated savanna where animals roam and visitors get the chance to see them up close.*

Getting There & Around

🚌 Buses shuttle between Animal Kingdom, Epcot, Disney's Hollywood Studios and the Transportation & Ticket Center near Magic Kingdom.

🚗 There's a big car park on-site.

Region Map on p86

Bengal tiger, Maharajah Jungle Trek (p87) © DISNEY

Top Experience 📷

Get Lost in Pandora – The World of Avatar

Welcome to the Valley of Mo'ara, where floating islands and the beautifully lush vegetation leave you in no doubt that this is a land far away from earth – 4.3 light years away. to be exact. This extraordinary land – and its two different but equally fabulous rides – is James Cameron and Disney imagineers at their absolute best.

◎ **MAP P86, B5**

www.disneyworld.com

Animal Kingdom

theme-park admission required

🕑 9am-6pm, hours vary

🚌 Disney

Avatar: Flight of Passage

Soar above Pandora atop a banshee on Avatar: Flight of Passage. After a pre-flight briefing explaining the concept of pairing with a banshee, you and 15 other cadets enter a chamber where you each strap into a vehicle (that looks vaguely like a motorcycle), put on your 3D goggles and then set off.

The jungle landscapes and seascapes feel completely real, and for added authenticity you can smell the faint must of the undergrowth and, as you skim the surface of the water, feel a light splash on your face. The seat pulsating beneath you gives the sensation of the banshee 'breathing' – just another layer of magic that helps you immerse completely into the experience. This is one of the best and most immersive rides of any theme park, anywhere.

Na'vi River Journey

This slow meander through the bioluminescent world of Pandora is short on thrills but very high on beauty: over 4½ minutes in a four-seater boat you drift past glowing flora and mysterious fauna. The ride climaxes in an encounter with the Na'vi Shaman of Songs, Pandora's life force, wonderfully rendered in audio-animatronics.

Pandora at Night

Pandora is beautiful during the day, but its otherworldly qualities really come out after sunset, when the bioluminescence makes you feel even more like you're on an alien planet. Which, of course, you are.

★ **Top Tips**

○ Avatar: Flight of Passage and Na'vi River Journey are incredibly popular, so you'll want to use your FastPass+ (booked as far in advance as possible), but as they're both Tier A options, you can only pick one on any given day.

○ Avatar: Flight of Passage has a height restriction of 44in.

✕ **Take a Break**

You can create your own bowl in the Pandora-themed **Satu'li Canteen** (www.disneyworld.com; Animal Kingdom; mains $13-18; ⏱11am-closing; 🖥Disney) – just pick a protein, base and sauce.

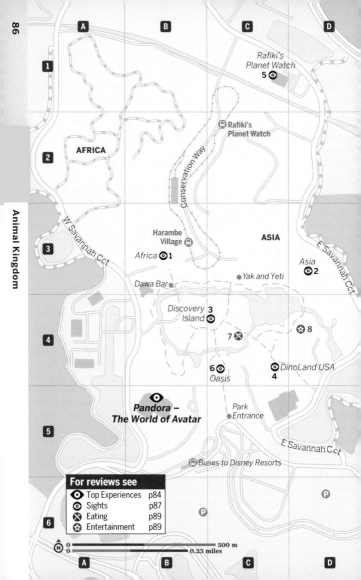

A B C D

1

Rafiki's
Planet Watch
5

🛉 Rafiki's
Planet Watch

2

AFRICA

Conservation Way

Harambe
Village 🏠 ASIA

Africa 🎯1

Asia
🎯2

Dawa Bar ●

Yak and Yeti ●

3

W Savannah Cct

E Savannah Cct

Discovery 3
Island 🎯

7 🍴

⭐ 8

4

6🎯
Oasis

🎯 DinoLand USA
4

Pandora –
The World of Avatar

🎯

Park
Entrance ●

5

E Savannah Cct

🚌 Buses to Disney Resorts

📍

For reviews see
🎯 Top Experiences   p84
🎯 Sights   p87
🍴 Eating   p89
⭐ Entertainment   p89

6

Ⓝ 0   500 m
   0   0.25 miles

A B C D

Sights

Africa   AREA

 MAP P86, B3

Board a jeep and ride through the African savanna on **Kilimanjaro Safaris**, pausing to look at zebras, lions, giraffes and more, all seemingly roaming free. This is one of the Animal Kingdom's most popular attractions, so come early or use your FastPass+.

Most of the park's live entertainment options are in Africa, including the long-running **Festival of the Lion King**, a song-and-dance performance based on the popular Disney animation set in its own theater. The **Gorilla Falls Exploration Trail** passes gorillas, hippos, a great bat display and a hive of naked mole rats – nothing more than you'd find in any zoo, but those mole rats sure are cute. (www.disneyworld.com; Animal Kingdom; theme-park admission required; ⊙9am-6pm, hours vary; ☐Disney)

Asia   AREA

2 ⊙ MAP P86, D3

Home to two of Animal Kingdom's three most popular rides: **Expedition Everest**, a great roller coaster with a yeti twist, and **Kali River Rapids**, a water ride.

Owls, peregrine falcons and many other birds dazzle audiences at **Flights of Wonder**. It's got some cheesy dialogue, but the animals are spectacular as they zoom around over your head on cue.

Maharajah Jungle Trek is a self-guided path past Bengal

Animal Kingdom Sights

Kilimanjaro Safaris, Africa

tigers, huge fruit bats and Komodo dragons. (www.disneyworld.com; Animal Kingdom; theme-park admission required; ⏰9am-6pm, hours vary; 🚉Disney)

Discovery Island AREA

3 ◉ MAP P86, C4

The centrepiece of this land (and of the whole park) is the **Tree of Life**, a carefully constructed baobab tree that's 14 stories high and carved with over 325 animals. Paths at the base lead to the *Bugs' Life*–themed **It's Tough to Be a Bug!**, a 4D movie that includes periods of darkness, dry ice and flashing lights. It's a lot of fun, but little 'uns may find it all a bit too scary. (www.disneyworld.com; Animal Kingdom; theme-park admission required; ⏰9am-6pm, hours vary; 🚉Disney)

DinoLand USA AREA

4 ◉ MAP P86, C4

This bizarre dinosaur-themed section seems more like a tired carnival than Disney Magic, with garish plastic dinosaurs, midway games and 'Trilo-Bite' snacks, but **DINOSAUR** is a really fun jeep ride with a *Jurassic Park* twist. Be warned – there's plenty of mayhem and panic, and you barely escape the menacing Carnotaurus and the crash of the meteor. (www.disneyworld.com; Animal Kingdom; theme-park admission required; ⏰9am-6pm, hours vary; 🚉Disney)

Disney Parades, Fireworks & Light Shows

It takes a little bit of planning to coordinate your schedule to hit Disney's parades and nighttime spectaculars. Note that times vary according to day and season. In addition to the following highlights, check www.disneyworld.com for other holiday celebrations and specialty parties.

Festival of Fantasy (p65) Elaborate floats and dancing characters, including Dumbo, Peter Pan and Sleeping Beauty.

Disney Enchantment (p52) This fireworks and light-show extravaganza features projections extending from Cinderella Castle all the way down Main Street, USA; the grand finale to many a visit.

Fantasmic (p73) A water, music and light show featuring Mickey Mouse as the Sorcerer's Apprentice from *Fantasia* using all kinds of wizardry to defeat a cast of Disney villains.

Mickey's Not-So-Scary Halloween Party (p65) With 'all the treats and no tricks', this Halloween pageant haunts Magic Kingdom on select evenings in fall.

Rafiki's Planet Watch ZOO

5 ⊙ MAP P86, C1

Veterinarians care for sick and injured animals at the **Conservation Station**. You can check out pet sheep and goats at **Affection Section**. On the **Habitat Habit!** trail check out the adorable, fist-sized tamarin monkeys. But ultimately, the **Wildlife Express Train** you take to get here might just be the best part of this Disney enigma. (www.disneyworld.com; Animal Kingdom; theme-park admission required; ⏱9am-6pm, hours vary; 🚻; 🚊Disney)

Oasis ZOO

6 ⊙ MAP P86, C4

Oasis is the first themed section of Animal Kingdom. It has cool critters, including a giant anteater, but it's best to move along to other attractions and pause to enjoy the animals on your way out. (www.disneyworld.com; Animal Kingdom; theme-park admission required; ⏱9am-6pm, hours vary; 🚻; 🚊Disney)

Eating

Flame Tree Barbecue BARBECUE $$

7 🍴 MAP P86, C4

Counter-service barbecue ribs and chicken; a favorite with in-the-know Disney fans. (www.disneyworld.com; Animal Kingdom; mains $12-17, theme-park admission required; ⏱11am-park closing; 📶🚻; 🚊Disney)

Quick Bite or Beverage

Head to **Yak & Yeti** (Map p86, C3; 📞407-824-9384; www.disney world.com; Animal Kingdom; mains $20-36, theme-park admission required; ⏱11am-park closing) in Asia for surprisingly good Asian fare, or grab a cold beer at the thatch-roofed **Dawa Bar** (Map p86, B3; www.disneyworld. com; Animal Kingdom; theme-park admission required; ⏱11am-park closing) in Harambe Village.

Entertainment

Finding Nemo: the Musical PERFORMING ARTS

8 ⭐ MAP P86, D4

Arguably the best show at Walt Disney World® and a favorite of both kids and adults, this sophisticated musical theater performance features massive and elaborate puppets on stage and down the aisles, incredible set design and fantastic acting.

The music was composed by Robert Lopez and Kristen Anderson-Lopez, who also wrote *Frozen*'s Academy Award–winning 'Let It Go,' and the spectacular puppets were created by Michael Curry, the creative and artistic force behind the puppets in Broadway's *The Lion King*. (www. disneyworld.com; Animal Kingdom; theme-park admission required; ⏱several shows daily; 🚻; 🚊Disney)

Universal Orlando Resort & Greater Orlando Regions

Universal Studios (p93)
Thrillingly imaginative representations of favorite cinematic worlds, including Harry Potter, Minions, the Simpsons and Transformers.

Wizarding World of Harry Potter – Diagon Alley
Wizarding World of Harry Potter – Hogsmeade

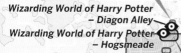

Downtown Orlando (p129)
Pedestrian-friendly neighborhood with some excellent restaurants, lively nightlife and a lovely city park.

Volcano Bay (p115)
Relax on the sandy beach, float down the river or up the adrenaline with a thrilling aqua coaster or a near-vertical water slide.

Islands of Adventure (p105)
Over-the-top, honest-to-goodness fun, with incredible roller coasters, Harry Potter's Hogsmeade and all the laughs of Toon Lagoon.

International Drive (p121)
Orlando's tourist hub, filled with restaurants, bars, stores and sights.

Explore Universal Orlando Resort & Greater Orlando

If Walt Disney World® is about finding the child in all of us, Universal Orlando Resort is all about our inner teenager. With three parks and a dining and entertainment district, Universal Orlando Resort is also smaller and much easier to navigate. Down off the coasters, Orlando proper offers a fabulous dining and nightlife scene, a wealth of museums and performing arts venues, and a number of outstanding experiences slightly further afield.

Explore ◉

Universal Studios

Universal Studios' simulation-heavy rides and shows are dedicated to silver-screen and TV icons. You can visit the Simpsons in Springfield, explore Diagon Alley and face all kinds of challenges with a host of favorites, from Minions to Transformers. Simulators and 3D rides dominate, but you'll also find two of the best traditional coasters in Orlando.

The Short List

○ **Hollywood Rip Ride Rockit (p97)** *High-thrill coaster with lots of loops, drops and a rip-roaring soundtrack.*

○ **Revenge of the Mummy (p97)** *Anger Imhotep at your peril on this indoor coaster that twists through the darkness.*

○ **Wizarding World of Harry Potter – Diagon Alley (p94)** *Thrilling rides and retail wonderland: theme-park creativity at its technical and imaginative best.*

○ **Moe's Tavern (p102)** *Who hasn't wanted to visit Homer's favorite watering hole in Springfield?*

○ **Universal Orlando's Cinematic Celebration (p103)** *A nighttime spectacular with lights, fountains and roaring dinosaurs.*

Getting There & Around

🚌 All buses stop by the entrance to CityWalk.

🚊 Connects CityWalk with four resort hotels.

🚕 Taxis stop at the car park by CityWalk.

🚗 Parking $25 a day (free after 6pm).

Region Map on p96

Top Experience
Make Magical Memories in Diagon Alley

The rickety street of Diagon Alley, lined with twisty, towering shops and – at one end – the imposing entrance to Gringotts Bank (protected by a huge dragon) is the stuff Harry Potter fans dream of. Inside the bank is the land's thrilling ride, but it's the range of themed shops and magical touches that make it special.

⊙ **MAP P96, B2**

www.universalorlando.com

theme-park admission required

⊙ from 9am

🚌 Lynx 21, 37 or 40

Harry Potter & the Escape from Gringotts

After walking through Gringotts Bank (pictured) and its marvellous collection of animatronic goblins, you get into the ride vehicle and go on a 3D journey into the bank's deepest recesses, despite the best efforts of Bellatrix Lestrange to stop you from going any further. Eventually, he-who-shall-not-be-named joins her, but have no fear: on your side is a pretty formidable, scaly fire-breathing creature. A great ride, and the simulations are gentler on your stomach than Harry Potter and the Forbidden Journey.

Ollivander's

Ollivander's have been 'makers of fine wands since 382 BC' and this shop is in its correct place according to the books. Buy all kinds of wands (both interactive and normal), but the real treats are its multiple choosing chambers, where a lucky someone (usually a child) is chosen for a wand-selecting ceremony that involves a bit of impressive jiggery-pokery. As you wait for the show, look out for the self-sweeping broom. Note: if you or your young one does get picked, you have to buy the wand in order to keep it.

Hogwarts Express

The Hogwarts Express connects Diagon Alley in Universal Studios to Hogsmeade in Islands of Adventure. It is literally a train, rather than a ride in the traditional sense, but the view out your compartment window is, indeed, magical! Live the wonderfully imaginative 'real' scenes with some special effect character 'appear-ances' along the way. (Enough said: we won't spoil the trip.)

While you can enter each area from within the respective parks with a one-park admission ticket, you must purchase a park-to-park ticket to ride the Hogwarts Express between Diagon Alley and Hogsmeade.

★ Top Tips

o If you're not a guest in a Universal resort and don't have early admission, lines for Harry Potter and the Escape from Gringotts are shorter around lunchtime or late afternoon.

o The Ukrainian Ironbelly dragon atop Gringotts Bank puts on a fire-breathing show every 15 minutes or so (unless it's too windy); you'll hear a low rumble before he does.

✕ Take a Break

Go for a filling, English-style school lunch at the Hogwarts-themed Leaky Cauldron (p100), but you might have to wait in line to get served.

Universal Studios

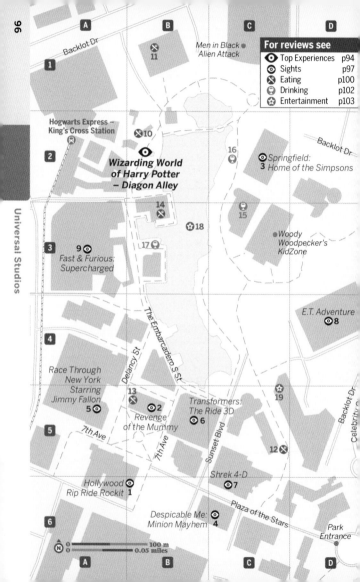

Backlot Dr

1

Men in Black
Alien Attack

11

For reviews see

◉	Top Experiences	p94
◉	Sights	p97
✕	Eating	p100
☕	Drinking	p102
★	Entertainment	p103

Hogwarts Express –
King's Cross Station

✕**10**

2

◉
**Wizarding World
of Harry Potter
– Diagon Alley**

16
☕

Backlot Dr

◉Springfield:
3 Home of the Simpsons

14
✕

☕
15

★**18**

3

9◉
*Fast & Furious:
Supercharged*

17☕

●Woody
Woodpecker's
KidZone

4

E.T. Adventure
◉**8**

The Embarcadero S St

*Race Through
New York
Starring
Jimmy Fallon*
5◉

13
✕

Delancy St

◉**2**
*Revenge
of the Mummy*

*Transformers:
The Ride 3D*
◉**6**

★
19

Backlot Dr

Celebrity Dr

5

7th Ave

7th Ave

Sunset Blvd

12✕

Hollywood ◉
Rip Ride Rockit **1**

Shrek 4-D
◉**7**

Plaza of the Stars

6

Despicable Me: ◉
Minion Mayhem **4**

Park
Entrance

Ⓝ 0 _____ 100 m
0 _____ 0.05 miles

Sights

Hollywood
Rip Ride Rockit
RIDE

◎ MAP P96, B6

This high-thrill coaster is not for the faint-hearted. You *Rip* up to 65mph, *Ride* 17 stories above the theme park and down a crazy-steep drop, and *Rockit* to your choice of song from a menu in your seat. You can get a video of the whole ride to see how calm you were throughout! (www.universalorlando.com; Universal Orlando Resort, Universal Studios; theme-park admission required; ⊙9am-6pm, hours vary; ⦷Lynx 21, 37 or 40)

Revenge of the Mummy
RIDE

◎ MAP P96, B5

One of the best rides in the park combines roller-coaster speed and twists with in-your-face special effects. Head deep into ancient Egyptian catacombs in near pitch black, but don't anger Imhotep the mummy – in his wrath he flings you past fire, water and more. (www.universalorlando.com; Universal Orlando Resort, Universal Studios; theme-park admission required; ⊙9am-6pm, hours vary; ⦷Lynx 21, 37 or 40)

Springfield:
Home of the Simpsons
AREA

◎ MAP P96, C2

In 2013 Universal opened *Simpsons*-themed Springfield, home to that iconic American TV family. Hang at Moe's Tavern, grab

The Lands of Universal Studios ⓘ

The park is divided into eight areas – **Hollywood**, **New York**, **Production Central**, **San Francisco**, **Springfield: Home of the Simpsons**, **Woody Woodpecker's KidZone**, **World Expo** and **Wizarding World of Harry Potter – Diagon Alley** – but the constant arrival of new rides means that most of the rides are no longer thematically connected to their respective lands.

doughnuts at Lard Lad, and meet Krusty the Clown, Sideshow Bob and the Simpson family themselves. The child-friendly **Kang & Kodos' Twirl & Hurl** offers an interactive twist to whirling, and don't miss the **Simpsons Ride** (Express Pass).

It's one of the best simulated experiences at Universal, a highlight even if you're not a *Simpsons* fan. Kids will want to try Springfield's signature drink, a bubbling and steaming Flaming Moe that rivals the theming fun of Harry Potter's Butterbeer and tastes surprisingly good! Sure, it's just an orange soda, but it's a pretty cool orange soda, the cup makes a good souvenir, and in the eyes of an eight-year-old, it's worth every cent of those nine dollars. (www.universalorlando.com; Universal Studios; theme-park admission required; ⊙9am-6pm, hours vary; ⦷; ⦷Lynx 21, 37 or 40)

Despicable Me: Minion Mayhem

RIDE

4 ◉ MAP P96, C6

Fans of *Despicable Me* won't want to miss the chance to become one of Gru's minions in this 3D simulated ride, one of Universal's best 3D experiences. There's lots of silliness, in the best of Minion traditions, and there's nothing particularly scary. Note that even Express Pass lines can soar upwards from 30 minutes, so come first thing. (www.universalorlando. com; Universal Orlando Resort, Universal Studios; theme-park admission required; ☉9am-6pm, hours vary; 🚌Lynx 21, 37 or 40)

Race Through New York Starring Jimmy Fallon

RID

5 ◉ MAP P96, A5

You don't have to be a fan of *The Tonight Show* to get a kick out of this 3D simulator ride that sees you race host Jimmy Fallon through the streets of New York and then up to the moon. The pre-ride experience, where you're serenaded by the Ragtime Gals and have a meet-and-greet with Hashtag the Panda, is as good as

Best Universal Orlando Resort Rides & Experiences for Kids

One Fish, Two Fish, Red Fish, Blue Fish Ride a Seussian fish around, slowly up and down, with just enough spin to thrill.

Caro-Seuss-al Hop on a fanciful Seuss character.

Cat in the Hat (p110) Classic ride through a storybook.

High in the Sky Seuss Trolley Train Ride Soar gently over the park.

If I Ran the Zoo Colorful interactive play area with water-spurting triggers.

Me Ship, the Olive Kids crawl, climb and squirt on Popeye's playground ship and zoom down tunnel waterslides.

Popeye & Bluto's Bilge-Rat Barges (p111) Float, twist, bump and giggle along on a circular raft – you will get drenched!

Hogwarts (p107) Little (and big) ones too young for the scary Harry Potter and the Forbidden Journey ride can walk through the magical charms of the famous wizardry school. The separate line for this isn't marked, so ask the accommodating Universal folks. Other kid-friendly highlights in the Wizarding World of Harry Potter are Ollivander's Wand Shop (10-minute show) and family coaster **Flight of the Hippogriff**.

Revenge of the Mummy (p97)

the ride itself. (www.universalorlando. om; Universal Orlando Resort, Univer- al Studios; ⊗9am-6pm, hours vary; 🚌Lynx 21, 37 or 40)

Transformers: The Ride 3D
RIDE

◉ MAP P96, B5

Get into the transport, don your 3D glasses and almost immediately you're catapulted into the middle of an epic battle to save the planet. Autobots including Optimus Prime and Bumblebee go head-to-head with nasty Decepticons as you whirl, bash, rise and fall. The effects are excellent and you'll be relieved the Autobots win. (www. universalorlando.com; Universal Studios; theme-park admission required; ⊗9am- pm, hours vary; 🚌Lynx 21, 37 or 40)

Shrek 4-D
RIDE

7 ◉ MAP P96, C6

Shrek and Donkey try to save Princess Fiona from a dragon. And that dragon is fierce, probably too fierce for tiny tots – it pops out at you with red eyes, spitting fire into your face. Unfortunately, the nonsensical preshow spiel goes on too long. Still, lines are long so use Express Pass. (www.universalorlando. com; Universal Orlando Resort, Universal Studios; theme-park admission required; ⊗9am-6pm, hours vary; 🚌Lynx 21, 37 or 40)

E.T. Adventure
RIDE

8 ◉ MAP P96, D4

This is one of Universal's classic rides and one for the nostalgia seekers. For some people, *E.T.* is

Other Universal Rides

In World Expo, the attraction is **Men in Black Alien Attack** (Map p96, C1; www.universal orlando.com; Universal Studios; theme-park admission required; ⏰9am-6pm, hours vary; 🚍Lynx 21, 37 or 40), a 3D interactive video game that is a lot of fun but not at all scary. Your car swings and spins through a danger-laden downtown Manhattan, with all kinds of silly-looking aliens everywhere, and you aim your lasers and shoot away to rack up points.

In **Woody Woodpecker's KidZone** (Map p96, C3; www.universalorlando.com; Universal Studios; theme-park admission required; ⏰9am-6pm, hours vary; 🚍Lynx 21, 37 or 40), you'll find kid-friendly shows and rides, a fantastic water-play area and supercool foam-ball cannons – a favorite with the eight-and-under crowd.

Universal. Jump aboard the flying bicycle and assist E.T. to save the planet. Dodge the baddies while soaring into the stars and into E.T.'s magical world. Sure it might be dated compared to some hi-tech 'competitors,' but it's sweet. And who, after all, can resist a shriveled little alien? (www.universalorlando. com; Universal Studios; theme-park admission required; ⏰from 9am; 🚍Lynx 21, 37 or 40)

Fast & Furious: Supercharged

RID

9 ◉ MAP P96, A3

After checking out a couple of the cars that featured in the $5-billion franchise, and a quick recap of the films' basic premise, you board the 'party bus' and soon find yourself in a chase that gets pretty fast, if not all that furious. The 4K projections are pretty good, but they pale in comparison to the immersive 3D of Skull Island: Reign of Kong in Islands of Adventure. (www. universalorlando.com; Universal Orland Resort, Universal Studios; theme-park admission required; ⏰9am-6pm, hour vary; 🚍Lynx 21, 37 or 40)

Eating

Leaky Cauldron

BRITISH $

10 ✖ MAP P96, B2

Wizard servers in marvelous Harr Potter surrounds with classic English breakfasts, shepherd's pie, Guinness beef stew and sticky toffee pudding. You order fast-foo style and the food is brought to your table – refectory of course, à la Potteresque boarding-school experience. No surprise, but this is one of the most popular restaurants in the whole park. Be prepared to wait.

The only drinks are Potter-themed delights, including non-alcoholic Peachtree Fizzing Tea an Fishy Green Ale, as well as dark ale Wizard's Brew and the malty Drag on Scale. (www.universalorlando.com

Universal Studios; mains $12-22, theme-park admission required; ⏱8am-park closing; 🚌Lynx 21, 37 or 40)

Florean Fortescue's Ice-Cream Parlour   ICE CREAM $

1 🍴 MAP P96, B1

In *Harry Potter and the Prisoner of Azkaban,* young Harry spends several weeks living at the Leaky Cauldron and Florean Fortescue gives him free ice cream whenever he pops into the store. His bright and charming shop, just across from the fire-spewing dragon on top of Gringotts Bank, is now open to muggles.

Bizarre and delectable flavors include Butterbeer, sticky toffee pudding and clotted cream, as well as pumpkin juice. (www.universalorlandoresort.com; Diagon Alley, Universal Studios; ice cream $5-10, theme-park admission required; ⏱park opening-1hr before park closing; 🚌Lynx 21, 37 or 40)

Mel's Drive-In   BURGERS $

12 🍴 MAP P96, C5

Based on the movie *American Graffiti,* this rockin' rollin' joint features classic cars and performing bands outside, '50s-diner style inside. This is a fast-food eatery, not very different really from your standard well-known burger joint, but it's a lot more fun! (www.universalorlando.com; Universal Studios; mains $13-20, theme-park admission required; ⏱11am-park closing; 👶; 🚌Lynx 21, 37 or 40, 🚆Universal)

Finnegan's Bar & Grill   PUB FOOD $$

13 🍴 MAP P96, B5

An Irish pub with live acoustic music plopped into the streets

Interactive Wands

Wands at Universal Orlando's Wizarding World of Harry Potter come in two varieties: interactive ($55) and noninteractive ($49). Interactive wands, including Hermione's and Harry's, can be used in both Diagon Alley and Hogsmeade to activate magical windows and displays. Make it rain down on an umbrella, illuminate lanterns, watch the marionettes dance. They can be a bit touchy to get used to – use small, gentle movements, and if you have trouble, ask a nearby wizard for help.

Gold medallions on the ground indicate spots where you can cast your spells, and how to move your wand to cast the spell, and each wand comes with a map. Some secret spell locations, however, aren't marked at all, either on the map or by a gold medallion, but we're not telling where they are. Hint: secret spells respond to a triangle swoop.

Universal Orlando's Cinematic Celebration

of New York. Serves Cornish beef pasties and Scotch eggs, as well as Harp, Bass and Guinness on tap. Annoyingly (as with many establishments, it seems), the prices are not shown on the outside menu. (📞407-224-3613; www.universal orlando.com; Universal Studios; mains $15-26, theme-park admission required; ⏰11am-1hr before park closes; 🛜♿; 🚌Lynx 21, 37 or 40)

Lombard's Seafood Grille
SEAFOOD $$

 14 🍴 MAP P96, B3

A more upmarket experience (and good for older folk). Features carpet and tile floors, a huge fish tank and a solid seafood menu. It's a calming respite from Universal

Orlando's energy, and the prices are, well, at least not astronomical. (📞407-224-6401; www.universal orlando.com; Universal Studios; mains $17-28, theme-park admission required ⏰11am-1hr before park closes; 🛜♿; 🚌Lynx 21, 37 or 40)

Drinking

Moe's Tavern
BAR

15 🍺 MAP P96, C3

Brilliantly themed *Simpsons* bar with Isotopes memorabilia, the Love Tester and Bart Simpson crank-calling the red rotary phone; it's as if you walked straight into your TV to find yourself at Homer's favorite neighborhood joint. Buy a Krusty Burger from the neighboring food court and sidle up for a Duff Beer, Duff Lite or Duff Dry. (www.universalorlando.com; Springfield, Universal Studios; drinks $3-9, theme-park admission required; ⊙11am-park closing; 🛜; 🚍Lynx 21, 37 or 40)

Duff Brewery BAR

16 🚻 MAP P96, C2

Outdoor lagoonside bar serving Homer Simpson's beer of choice, on tap or by the bottle, and Springfield's signature Flaming Moe. Look for the topiary Seven Duffs out front – Tipsy, Queasy, Surly, Sleazy, Edgy, Dizzy and Remorseful. (www.universalorlando.com; Springfield, Universal Studios; snacks $6-15, theme-park admission required; ⊙11am-park closing; 🛜; 🚍Lynx 21, 37 or 40)

Chez Alcatraz BAR

17 🚻 MAP P96, B3

Frozen mojitos, flatbread and homemade potato chips on the waterfront at Fisherman's Wharf. With the sound of the boats jingling at the docks, views over the water to the *Simpsons*-themed Springfield, and Bruce the infamous shark from *Jaws* dangling as a photo-op, this little outdoor bar makes a pleasant spot to kick back and relax. (www.universalorlando. com; Universal Studios, San Francisco; theme-park admission required; ⊙noon-park closing; 🛜; 🚍Lynx 21, 37 or 40)

Entertainment

Universal Orlando's Cinematic Celebration CINEMA

18 ⭐ MAP P96, B3

The 40ft-wide water curtains pull back on this nighttime spectacular that uses 120 water fountains, fireworks and crystal clear projections of some of Universal's most popular attractions, including *Jurassic World, Despicable Me, Fast & Furious, E.T.* and *Harry Potter.* The show takes place over the lagoon in Universal Studios as 6500 people gather on the grass at Central Park. (🖉dining reservations 407-224-7554; www.universalorlando. com; Universal Studios; theme-park admission required; ⊙evenings, times vary; 🚍Lynx 21, 37 or 40)

Universal Orlando's Horror Make-Up Show LIVE PERFORMANCE

19 ⭐ MAP P96, C5

A lively and very funny insight into how make-up artists create film monsters, this terrific 25-minute show pulls the bandages back and reveals how fake wounds, severed limbs and all that movie gore are created. The light-touch comedy means that even pre-teens can handle it, although you might want to make it clear that it's not real. (www.universalorlando.com; Universal Studios; theme-park admission required; ⊙9am-6pm, hours vary; 🚍Lynx 21, 37 or 40)

Explore ⊛
Islands of Adventure

Right from the entrance, Islands of Adventure is all about a no-holds-barred, laugh-out-loud kind of fun. Marvel Super Hero Island is packed with thrill rides and hair-raising coasters; Toon Lagoon is like stepping into a cartoon; and then there's the Wizarding World of Harry Potter – Hogsmeade, a game changer when it opened in 2010 and still as wonderful today.

The Short List

○ **Wizarding World of Harry Potter – Hogsmeade (p106)** *Explore the cobbled streets of Harry Potter's Hogsmeade, a world-class theme-park experience.*

○ **Incredible Hulk Coaster (p109)** *Literally incredible, this coaster is a twisting, turning, high-speed thriller.*

○ **Amazing Adventures of Spider-Man (p109)** *Fabulous simulator ride where you come face-to-face with Spidey's nefarious enemies.*

○ **Hagrid's Magical Creatures Motorbike Adventure (p107)** *Hogsmeade's newest coaster throws up some delightful surprises along the way.*

○ **Harry Potter & the Forbidden Journey (p107)** *Fly through Hogwarts on this extraordinary simulated ride.*

Getting There & Around

🚌 All buses stop by the entrance to CityWalk.

⛴ Connects CityWalk with four resort hotels.

🚕 Taxis stop at the car park by CityWalk.

🚗 Parking is $25 a day (free after 6pm).

Region Map on p108

Hagrid's Magical Creatures Motorbike Adventure (p107)

Top Experience 📷

Wander the Wizarding World of Harry Potter at Hogsmeade

Poke along the cobbled streets of Hogsmeade, sip frothy Butterbeer, munch on Cauldron Cakes and mail a card via Owl Post, all in the shadow of Hogwarts Castle (pictured). The detail and authenticity tickle the fancy at every turn, from the screeches of the mandrakes in the shop windows to the groans of Moaning Myrtle in the bathroom – keep your eyes peeled for magical happenings.

◎ MAP P108, C2

📞 407-363-8000

www.universalorlando.com

theme-park admission required

🕒 9am-6pm, hours vary

🚌 Lynx 21, 37 or 40

Harry Potter & the Forbidden Journey

Wind through the corridors of **Hogwarts**, past talking portraits, Dumbledore's office and other well-known locations, to one of the best rides in Orlando. You'll feel the cold chill of Dementors, escape a dragon attack, join a Quidditch match and soar over the castle with Harry, Hermione and Ron. Though it's not a fast-moving thrill ride, this is scary stuff. Little ones can enjoy the castle but sit out the ride with a parent in the Child Swap waiting room.

Hagrid's Magical Creatures Motorbike Adventure

Climb aboard Hagrid's motorcycle or sidecar and, with Hagrid's blessing, take a fast, fun coaster ride that includes a vertical tunnel leading to a backward helix and an unexpected but wonderfully enjoyable free-fall drop. Opened in 2019, this ride has quickly become a big highlight.

Flight of the Hippogriff

It's only a minute long, but this family friendly coaster is great for little kids (taller than 36in). It passes over Hagrid's Hut; listen for Fang's barks and don't forget to bow to Buckbeak!

Shopping in Hogsmeade

Find the perfect wand in the floor-to-ceiling shelves of **Ollivander's**, before popping into **Dervish & Banges** to find the appropriate robe and other magical supplies. Nearby **Filch's Emporium of Confiscated Goods** is another souvenir shop. Load up on Bertie Bott's Every Flavor Beans, Chocolate Frogs, Rock Cakes and other Harry Potter–inspired goodies at **Honeydukes** and then drop by the **Owl Post & Owlery** to send a card officially postmarked Hogsmeade.

★ Top Tips

o The single rider line for Harry Potter and the Forbidden Journey is hard to find; ask at the Hogwarts entrance.

o Ride Hagrid's Magical Creatures Motorbike Adventure as early as possible or just before the park closes.

o If you can, try not to ride Harry Potter and the Forbidden Journey on an empty stomach; if you feel queasy, look at your feet.

✗ Take a Break

Harry Potter–inspired fare at Three Broomsticks (p112) is filling, tasty and conveniently keeps you firmly in the Hogsmeade universe.

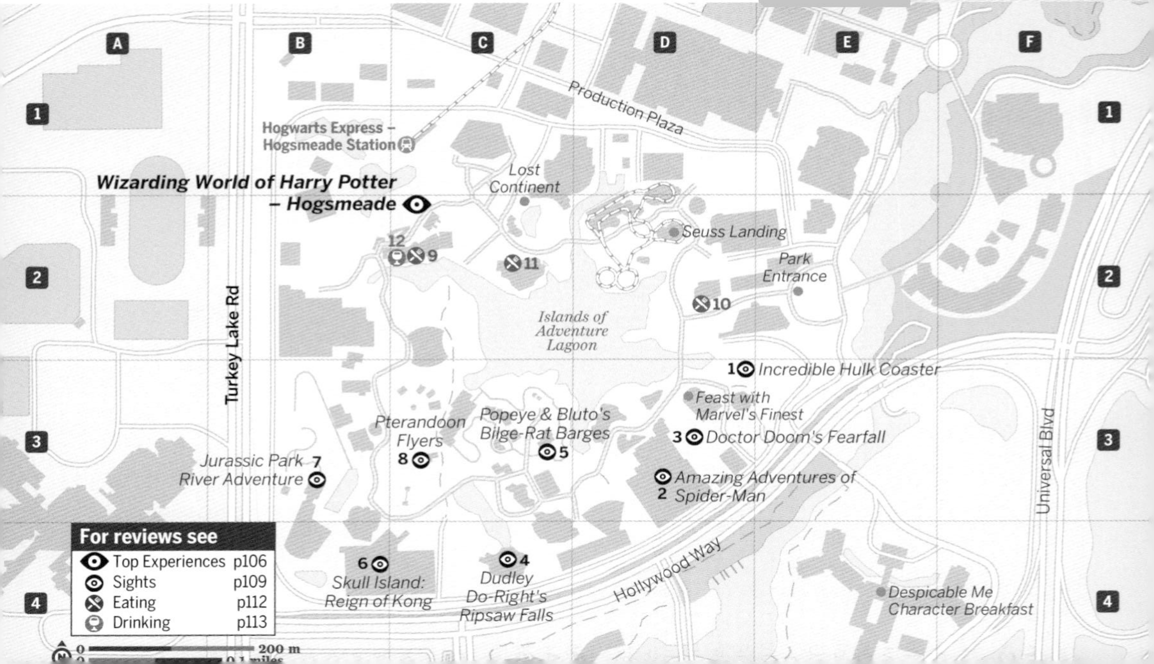

Islands of Adventure

Wizarding World of Harry Potter
– Hogsmeade

Hogwarts Express –
Hogsmeade Station

Hogsmeade

Turkey Lake Rd

Jurassic Park 7
River Adventure

Pteranodon
Flyers 8

Skull Island: 6
Reign of Kong

Popeye & Bluto's
Bilge-Rat Barges 5

Dudley
Do-Right's
Ripsaw Falls 4

Lost
Continent

Production Plaza

Seuss Landing

Park
Entrance

Islands of
Adventure Lagoon

Feast with
Marvel's Finest

Doctor Doom's Fearfall 3

Amazing Adventures of
Spider-Man 2

Incredible Hulk Coaster 1

Universal Blvd

Hollywood Way

Despicable Me
Character Breakfast

For reviews see

◉ Top Experiences	p106
◉ Sights	p109
✕ Eating	p112
Ⓓ Drinking	p113

200 m
0.1 miles

Sights

Incredible Hulk Coaster
MARVEL SUPERHERO ISLAND

🎯 MAP P108

Our favorite coaster across all three of Universal's parks starts with a takeoff that takes you from 0mph to 40mph in *two seconds*, followed by a quick twist and a 100ft drop. The rest of the ride is a mix of twists, turns and dives that replicate the g-force of a jet fighter. Absolutely fabulous stuff. (www.universalorlando.com; Universal Orlando Resort, Islands of Adventure; theme-park admission required; ⏲9am-6pm, hours vary; 🚌Lynx 21, 37 or 40)

Amazing Adventures of Spider-Man
MARVEL SUPERHERO ISLAND

2 🎯 MAP P108

One of the best simulator 4D rides in the park, this high-def, high-tech adventure pits you against some of Spider-Man's deadliest enemies while coursing through the streets of New York. You'll feel every bump, every blast of heat and a splash of water from Hydro-Man – but there's always Spidey to make sure you're OK. (www.universal orlando.com; Universal Orlando Resort, Islands of Adventure; theme-park admission required; ⏲9am-6pm, hours vary; 🚌Lynx 21, 37 or 40)

Avoiding the Harry Hordes ⓘ

Nothing will kill the excitement of going on your favourite ride more than having to wait for hours in line. Visit smart and you'll enjoy the magic without the stress.

○ Visit during low season. Don't go Christmas through early January, March, April or in summer. May, early September and early November see the lightest crowds.

○ Stay at a Universal Orlando Resort Hotel. Harry Potter attractions open one hour early for guests at all four on-site hotels.

○ Take advantage of Universal's 'return time' tickets. If the Wizarding World of Harry Potter does reach capacity, it only allows new guests to enter once others have left – this electronic ticket allows you to enjoy other attractions and return for entry within a specific window of time.

Doctor Doom's Fearfall
MARVEL SUPERHERO ISLAND

3 🎯 MAP P108

Doctor Doom has a plan for you, but first you must strap into his dastardly contraption. As you blast 200ft upwards with your feet dangling below you, his plan becomes

Other Islands of Adventure Areas to Explore

Lost Continent

Magic and myth from across the seas and the pages of fantasy books inspire this **mystical corner** (Map p108, C2; www.universal orlando.com; Universal Orlando Resort, Islands of Adventure; theme-park admission required; 9am-6pm, hours vary; Lynx 21, 37 or 40) of the park. Here you'll find dragons and unicorns, psychic readings and fortune-tellers. And don't be startled if that fountain talks to you as you walk past. The **Mystic Fountain** banters sassily, soaking children with its waterspouts when they least expect it and engaging them in silly conversation.

At the swashbuckling **Eighth Voyage of Sinbad Stunt Show** (Express Pass), Sinbad and his sidekick Kabob must rescue Princess Amoura from the terrible Miseria and, of course, Sinbad has to tumble and jump around to do it. Or head into the ancient Temple of Poseidon in **Poseidon's Fury** with an archaeologist who leads you deep into the temple...until you're 'trapped' in a massive battle with lasers, water and fireballs.

Seuss Landing

Anyone who has ever fallen asleep being read *Green Eggs and Ham* or learned to read with Sam-I-Am knows the world of Dr Seuss: the fanciful creatures, the lyrical names, the rhyming stories. In **Seuss Landing** (Map p108, D2; www.universalorlando.com; Islands of Adventure; theme-park admission required; 9am-6pm, hours vary; Lynx 21, 37 or 40), realized in magnificently designed 3D form, is Dr Seuss' imagination. The Lorax guards his truffula trees; Thing One and Thing Two make trouble; and creatures from all kinds of Seuss favorites adorn the shops and the rides.

Drink moose juice or goose juice; eat green eggs and ham; and peruse shelves of Dr Seuss books before riding through the **Cat in the Hat** or around and around on an elephant-bird from *Horton Hears a Who!*. Seuss Landing is one of the best places for little ones in all of Orlando's theme parks, bringing the spirit and energy of Dr Seuss' vision to life. So come on in, walk into his world and take a spin on a fish.

clear. The ride itself isn't nearly as scary as the apprehension that precedes it, but that's all part of the fun. (www.universalorlando. com; Univeral Resort Orlando, Islands of Adventure; theme-park admission required; 9am-6pm, hours vary; Lynx 21, 37 or 40)

Dudley Do-Right's
Ripsaw Falls
TOON LAGOON

4 ⊙ MAP P108

A flume ride through the Canadian
Rockies that ends in a big drop.
Does Dudley Do-Right rescue his
girlfriend Nell Fenwick from the
clutches of Snidely Whiplash?
Sure, why not? All we know is this
is a great ride that *will* leave you
wet. (www.universalorlando.com;
Universal Orlando Resort, Islands of
Adventure; theme-park admission
required; ⊙9am-6pm, hours vary;
🚌Lynx 21, 37 or 40)

Popeye & Bluto's
Bilge-Rat Barges
TOON LAGOON

5 ⊙ MAP P108

This whitewater rafting ride is
brilliant fun for the whole family,
but be prepared to get very, very
wet – the ride is designed so that
you do. (www.universalorlando.com;
Universal Orlando Resort, Islands of
Adventure; theme-park admission
required; ⊙9am-6pm, hours vary;
🚌Lynx 21, 37 or 40)

Skull Island:
Reign of Kong
SKULL ISLAND

6 ⊙ MAP P108

Board a trackless 72-seat, open-
sided vehicle 'driven' by a wise-
cracking animatronic tour guide
and head deep into Skull Island,
where high-tech 3D screens bring
its collection of oversized beasts
to life. The biggest threat comes
from a ferocious V-rex dinosaur...

or is it Kong himself? Suffice to
say, not for littlies. (www.universal
orlando.com; Islands of Adventure;
theme-park admission required;
⊙9am-6pm, hours vary; 🚌Lynx 21,
37 or 40)

Jurassic Park
River Adventure
JURASSIC PARK

7 ⊙ MAP P108

The journey starts innocuously
enough: you float past friendly
vegetarian dinosaurs, and all
seems well and good until...
things go wrong and those grass-
munchin' cuties are replaced with
the stuff of nightmares. To escape
the looming teeth of the giant
T-Rex, you plunge 85ft to the water
below. Little children might be
terrified by the creatures, the dark

Doctor Doom's Fearfall (p109)

and the plunge, but if yours are tough as nails they'll love it. (www.universalorlando.com; Universal Resort Orlando, Islands of Adventure; theme-park admission required; ⏰9am-6pm, hours vary; 🚹 🚍Lynx 21, 37 or 40)

Pterandoon Flyers

JURASSIC PARK

8 📍 MAP P108

At Pterandoon Flyers, kids fly over the lush landscape and robotic dinosaurs of Jurassic Park. Note that you must be between 36in and 56in tall to fly, and adults can't fly without a kid (also note: it sways quite severely; you don't just 'float' along). Waits can be upwards of an hour for the 80-second ride and there's no Express Pass. (www.

universalorlando.com; Universal Resort Orlando, Islands of Adventure; theme-park admission required; ⏰9am-6pm, hours vary; 🚍Lynx 21, 37 or 40)

Eating

Three Broomsticks

BRITISH $

9 🍴 MAP P108, C2

Fast-food-styled British fare inspired by Harry Potter, with tasty cottage (shepherd's) pie and Cornish pasties, and rustic wooden bench seating. There's also plenty of outdoor seating out back by the river. (www.universalorlando.com; Islands of Adventure; mains $12-18, theme-park admission required; ⏰9am-park closing; 🚹; 🚍Lynx 21, 37 or 40)

Butterbeer, Three Broomsticks

Confisco Grille & Backwater Bar

AMERICAN $$

10 ⊗ MAP P108, D2

Under-the-radar and often overlooked, the recommended Confisco Grille has outdoor seating, freshly made hummus, wood-oven pizzas and a full bar. Plant-based veggie or vegan options are available. (📞 407-224-4406; www.universalorlando.com; Islands of Adventure; mains $19-26, theme-park admission required; ⏰ 11am-4pm Mon-Thu, to 6pm Fri-Sun; ⚲ ♿; 🚌 Lynx 21, 37 or 40)

Mythos Restaurant

MEDITERRANEAN $$

11 ⊗ MAP P108, C2

Housed in an ornate underwater grotto with giant windows and running water and overlooking a lake, Mythos successfully combines Mediterranean flavors with tastes of Asian cuisine and a healthy dollop of American cooking. The menu changes seasonally but you can chomp on anything from pad Thai noodles to risotto. New plant-based options have been added to the menu. (📞 407-224-4534; www.universalorlando.com; Islands of Adventure; mains $19-34, theme-park admission required; ⏰ 11am-1hr before park closes; ⚲ ♿; 🚌 Lynx 21, 37 or 40)

Character Dining

🍽

You can have breakfast with Gru and the Minions every Saturday at the **Despicable Me Character Breakfast** (Map p108, E4; 📞 407-503-3463; www.universalorlando.com; 6300 Holly-wood Way, Royal Pacific Resort; adult/child $40/25; ⏰ seating times Sat 8am, 9.30am & 11am), or meet a handful of superheroes at the **Feast with Marvel's Finest** (Map p108, D3; www.universalorlando.com; Cafe 4, Islands of Adventure; adult/child $50/25, theme-park admission required; ⏰ 5pm Thu-Sun; 🚌 Lynx 21, 37 or 40).

Drinking

Hog's Head Pub

PUB

12 🍷 MAP P108, C2

Butterbeer, frozen or frothy, real beer on tap, pumpkin cider and more. Keep an eye on that hog over the bar – he's more real than you think! If the lines at the Butterbeer carts outside are too long, head inside. Same thing, same price. (www.universalorlando.com; Islands of Adventure, Universal Studios; drinks $4-8, theme-park admission required; ⏰ park opening-park closing; 🚌 Lynx 21, 37 or 40)

Explore ◈

Volcano Bay

Volcano Bay is a Polynesian-themed, 28-acre pleasure paradise of flumes, slides and rides designed around Krakatau, a 200ft volcano that dominates the park and is visible for miles around. Universal Orlando's third park was built to replace Wet 'n' Wild, but this is no ordinary splash-and-slide park — its 18 attractions set a new standard in water-based fun.

The Short List

∘ *Kala & Tai Nui Serpentine Body Slides (p117)* Fall through a trapdoor and slide to the bottom of the volcano.

∘ *Krakatau Aqua Coaster (p117)* The park's signature ride is a thrilling coaster that shoots through water like a toboggan.

∘ *Ko'okiri Body Plunge (p117)* The fastest way down the volcano is this near-vertical drop: are you brave enough?

Getting There & Around

🚌 Universal Orlando hotel guests can use the free shuttle bus from their hotel to the park; nonguests must get the shuttle from CityWalk.

🚗 Park at CityWalk ($25).

Region Map on p116

Waturi Beach (p119)

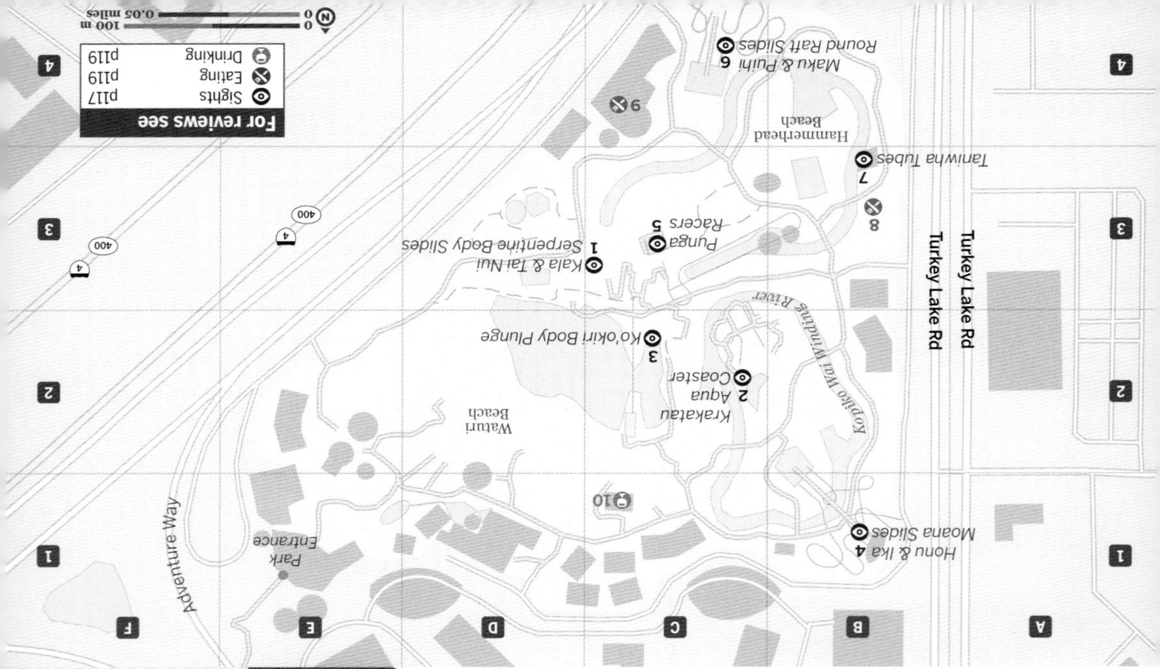

Volcano Bay

Adventure Way

Park Entrance

Waturi Beach

Ko'okiri Body Plunge 3

Krakatau Aqua Coaster 2

Kopiko Wai Winding River

Honu & Ika Moana Slides 4

Turkey Lake Rd

Turkey Lake Rd

Kala & Tai Nui Serpentine Body Slides 1

Punga Racers 5

Hammerhead Beach

Taniwha Tubes 7

Maku & Puihi Round Raft Slides 6

For reviews see	
⊙ Sights	p117
⊗⊗ Eating	p119
⊗⊗ Drinking	p119

100 m
0.05 miles

Sights

Kala & Tai Nui Serpentine Body Slides
RIDE

MAP P116, C3

The beating of the drums gets louder and more frenetic, and then the trapdoor is released – and you're sliding down a snaking tube that delivers you to the bottom of the volcano. You have a choice between a green and blue slide; the green one is slightly quicker. (www.universalorlando.com; Universal Orlando Resort, Volcano Bay; theme-park admission required; ⊙10am-6pm, hours vary; 🚌Universal)

Krakatau Aqua Coaster
RIDE

2 MAP P116, C2

Volcano Bay's signature ride is this coaster where you board a four-person canoe and then take off on a 60-second toboggan-style run that sees you rounding corners and shooting down straights at speed, all the while climbing and dropping for extra thrills. The launch effect is all thanks to linear induction motor technology, which makes this one of the best coasters in Orlando. (www.universalorlando.com; Universal Orlando Resort, Volcano Bay; theme-park admission required; ⊙10am-6pm, hours vary; 🚌Universal)

Ko'okiri Body Plunge
RIDE

3 MAP P116, C2

The tallest trapdoor plunge ride in North America is 208 steps up the towering volcano. It dizzyingly delivers you 125ft down to earth (well, to a splash pool) much more quickly than it took you to get up those steps. (www.universalorlando.com; Universal Orlando Resort, Volcano Bay; theme-park admission required; ⊙10am-6pm, hours vary; 🚌Universal)

Honu & Ika Moana Slides
RIDE

4 MAP P116, B1

These are two distinct slides operating from the same tower. You grab a multiperson raft and choose between Honu – a blue raft slide that sends you vertically up two huge walls before dumping you into a pool – and the green Ika Moana, a gentler version where

Krakatau Aqua Coaster

you twist your way down the tunnel. (www.universalorlando.com; Volcano Bay; theme-park admission required; ⏱10am-6pm, hours vary; 🚊Universal)

Punga Racers
RIDE

5 ◉ MAP P116, C3

Grab a manta-ray-shaped mat and race three of your friends (or anyone else) down a set of four enclosed slides. (www.universalorlando.com; Volcano Bay; theme-park admission required; ⏱10am-6pm, hours vary; 🚊Universal)

Maku & Puihi Round Raft Slides
RIDE

6 ◉ MAP P116, C4

A six-person raft plunges you through a series of bowls before finally dumping you into a pool at the bottom. Take your choice of slide: maku (the yellow one) means 'wet'; puihi (green) means 'wild' – a subtle tribute to Wet 'n' Wild, which Volcano Bay replaced. (www.universalorlando.com; Volcano Bay; theme-park admission required; ⏱10am-6pm, hours vary; 🚊Universal)

Taniwha Tubes
RIDE

7 ◉ MAP P116, B3

Climb to the top of the tower (adorned with Easter Island–type statues) for your choice of single- or double-rider slides. The green Tonga slide (on the far left) has more open-air sections. (www.universalorlando.com; Volcano Bay; theme-park admission required; ⏱10am-6pm, hours vary; 🚊Universal)

Maku & Puihi Round Raft Slides

Wristbands & Relaxation

TapuTapu Wristbands

All visitors are issued a 'TapuTapu' waterproof wristband, which you use to claim your spot in Volcano Bay's virtual lines, reserve lockers and make payments throughout the park. It needs to be linked to a credit card, either through the Universal Orlando website or its app. The wristbands also trigger some special effects, like the water cannons pointed at the Kopiko Wai Winding River or the water streams at the Tot Tiki Reef.

Lazing at Volcano Bay

Sure, there are thrill rides and slides, but Volcano Bay is also about maximum relaxation. **Waturi Beach**, which you come across as you come into the park, has real sand and is stocked with loungers and beach umbrellas. The **Kopiko Wai Winding River** is a gentle lazy river that does a loop around most of the park – grab a life vest and just float on.

Eating

Whakawaiwai Eats
AMERICAN $

3 🍴 MAP P116, B3

Pizzas, hot dogs, mac 'n' cheese... you get the picture. Great fillers after a few hours on the slides, but it also does healthy salads. (www. universalorlando.com; Volcano Bay; mains $13-17; theme-park admission required; ☺10am-6pm, hours vary; 🚈Universal)

Bambu
AMERICAN $$

9 🍴 MAP P116, C4

Burgers of every variety fill up the menu at this beach-shack-themed restaurant, probably the best in Volcano Bay. If you're looking for

healthy options, there's a delicious quinoa-edamame burger. (www. universalorlando.com; Volcano Bay; mains $12-20; theme-park admission required; ☺10am-6pm, hours vary; 🚈Universal)

Drinking

Dancing Dragons Boat Bar
COCKTAIL BAR

10 🍷 MAP P116, C1

This bar is designed to (vaguely) resemble a Chinese junk, but the cocktails are strictly tropical – and a mite sweet. The locally brewed Volcano Blossom beer is very tasty, though. (www.universalorlando. com; Volcano Bay; theme-park admission required; ☺10am-6pm, hours vary; 🚈Universal)

Explore ⊕
International Drive

I-Drive is Orlando's tourist hub, packed with restaurants (including the world's biggest McDonald's), bars, stores, accommodations and Orlando attractions both tired and new. It parallels I-4 to its east, stretching 17 miles from Orlando Premium Outlets south to World Dr, just east of Walt Disney World®. For the most part, this is Orlando tourism at full throttle.

The Short List

○ **WonderWorks (p123)** *Inside this upside-down building is a fabulous children's science center, arcade and amusement park, all in one.*

○ **SeaWorld (p125)** *Three of the best coasters in Florida are in this aquatic-themed park.*

○ **Sea Life (p124)** *Get up close and personal with a massive variety of marine life at this large aquarium.*

○ **Fun Spot America – Orlando (p124)** *An old-school theme park with a wooden roller coaster and lots of fun rides.*

○ **I-Drive NASCAR (p123)** *Channel your inner racer at this indoor track where the go-karts get up to 40mph.*

Getting There & Around
🚋 The I-Ride Trolley runs virtually the whole length of International Drive.

🚌 Lynx 8, 38, 42, 50 and 58 serve International Drive.

Neighbourhood Map on p122

Wheel at Icon Park (p124) NOAH DENSMORE/SHUTTERSTOCK ©

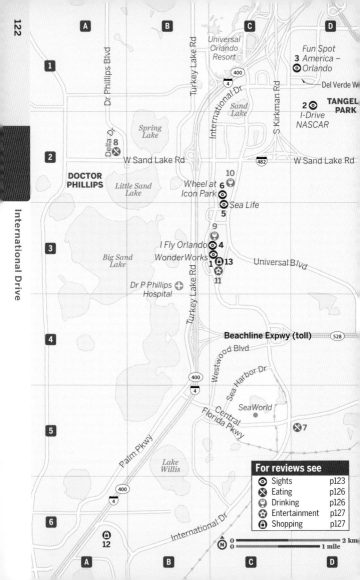

International Drive

A **B** **C** **D**

1

Dr Phillips Blvd

Turkey Lake Rd

Universal
Orlando
Resort

400

4

*Fun Spot
America –
Orlando* **3** ⊙

Del Verde W

2

Della Dr

8 ⊙

Spring
Lake

International Dr

*Sand
Lake*

S Kirkman Rd

2 ⊙
*I-Drive
NASCAR*

**TANGEL
PARK**

W Sand Lake Rd

482

W Sand Lake Rd

**DOCTOR
PHILLIPS**

*Little Sand
Lake*

10 🍴

Wheel at
Icon Park **6** ⊙

⊙ *Sea Life*
5

3

*Big Sand
Lake*

I Fly Orlando ⊙ **4**
WonderWorks ⊙ **9**
              🔒 **13**
1 ⭐
11

Universal Blvd

Dr P Phillips ✚
Hospital

4

Beachline Expwy (toll)

528

400

4

Westwood Blvd

Sea Harbor Dr

5

Central
Florida Pkwy

SeaWorld

❌ **7**

Palm Pkwy

*Lake
Willis*

6

400

4

12 🔒

International Dr

For reviews see	
⊙ Sights	p123
❌ Eating	p126
🍴 Drinking	p126
⭐ Entertainment	p127
🔒 Shopping	p127

Ⓝ 0 _____ 2 km
   0 _____ 1 mile

A **B** **C** **D**

Sights

WonderWorks   MUSEUM

⊙ MAP P122, C3

Housed in a hard-to-miss, upside-down building, this is a bright, loud, frenetic landmark, and is a cross between a children's museum, a video arcade and an amusement park. Several stories of interactive exhibits offer high-speed, multisensory education. Lie on a bed of nails, sit inside a hurricane simulator and so on.

Younger children may find the pulse disorienting and frightening, but older ones will probably enjoy the cool stuff there is to do. There's also a 36ft indoor ropes course, a 4D theater with changing shows, laser tag, and the nightly (and very funny) **Outta Control Magic Show**. (📞407-351-8800; www.wonderworksonline.com; 9067 International Dr; adult/child 4-12yr $36/27; ⊙9am-midnight; 🚻; 🚌Lynx 8, 38, 42, 🚃I-Ride Trolley Red Line Stop 18 or Green Line Stop 10)

I-Drive NASCAR   AMUSEMENT PARK

2 ⊙ MAP P122, D1

Inside a huge blue-and-yellow container building is the fastest indoor go-kart track in Florida, with speeds up to 45mph. Each race lasts around eight minutes and when you're done, there's a whole amusement arcade to explore before you decide that you really want to try and beat the track record. (📞407-581-9644; www.idrivenascar. com; 5228 Vanguard St; race adult/child

WonderWorks

$19/17; ⊙noon-10pm Mon-Thu, 11am-11pm Fri & Sat, 11am-10pm Sun; 🚍I-Ride Trolley Red/Green Lines Stop 4)

Fun Spot America – Orlando
AMUSEMENT PARK

3 ◉ MAP P122, D1

County-fair-like amusement park, with go-carts, kiddy rides, a wooden roller coaster and more. There's also a small section called 'Gator Spot,' an overflow area owned by **Gatorland** (📞407-855-5496; www.gatorland.com), with around 100 young 'gators. (📞407-363-3867; http://fun-spot.com; 5700 Fun Spot Way, International Dr; admission free, unlimited all-day rides $55; ⊙10am-midnight; 🚍I-Ride Trolley Red Line Stop 1, 2)

I Fly Orlando
ADVENTURE SPORTS

4 ◉ MAP P122, C3

This is as close as you'll get to skydiving without leaving the room. Suit up and take to the 12ft-high, 1000HP wind tunnel, where the effect is so realistic that skydiving clubs use the facility for training purposes. You can add a 'High Flight' experience to soar even higher and faster. It's fun and safe, even for kids as young as four. (📞407-337-4359; www.iflyworld.com; 8969 International Dr; 2-flight adult from $85, high flight extra $20; ⊙10am-7pm Sun-Thu, to 8pm Fri, to 9pm Sat; 👷; 🚍Lynx 8, 38, 42, 🚍I-Ride Trolley Red Line Stop 18 or Green Line Stop 10)

Sea Life
AQUARIUM

5 ◉ MAP P122, C3

Orlando's version of this global franchise dedicated to underwater marine life is divided into many themes, and has an educational, sustainable line to its exhibits, including talks and feeding sessions. The 360-degree glass tunnel is the highly promoted centerpiece. Combination tickets are available with the Wheel at Icon Park (below) and Madame Tussauds. (📞866-622-0607; www.visitsealife.com/orlando; 8449 International Dr, International Dr; adult/child $35/30; ⊙10am-9pm)

Wheel at Icon Park
AMUSEMENT PARK

6 ◉ MAP P122, C2

Orlando's massive Ferris wheel gives you bird's-eye views of the theme parks and the surrounding area. Greater Orlando is pretty flat, so visibility on clear days extends up to 50 miles as far as Cape Canaveral. iPads in the high-tech capsules help you locate all of the major landmarks. Check ahead as it sometimes closes for private events.

Combination tickets are available with **Madame Tussauds** (www.madametussauds.com/orlando) and Sea Life (above). (www.iconorlando.com; I-Drive 360, 8401 International Dr, International Drive; from $29; ⊙noon-10pm Sun-Thu, to 11pm Fri & Sat)

To See or Not to SeaWorld

SeaWorld (Map p122, C5; ☏ 407-545-5550; www.seaworldparks.com; 7007 Sea World Dr; $99, discounts online, prices vary daily; ⏱ 9am-8pm; 🚼 🐾; ☐ Lynx 8, 38, 50, 111, ☐ I-Ride Trolley Red Line Stop 28) is one of Orlando's largest theme parks. Its traditional drawcards were the live shows featuring trained dolphins, sea lions and killer whales, but the company is slowly pivoting away from these shows in reaction to the negative PR and falling visitor numbers that resulted from the 2013 documentary *Blackfish*, which alleged serious mistreatment of its captive orcas.

The film is a damning portrayal of the effects of keeping killer whales in captivity and charts the life of Tilikum, an orca at SeaWorld Orlando that was involved in the deaths of three people, including one of its trainers during a live show. Since its release, many animal welfare groups have come out in support of the film. Research by conservationists shows it is harmful and stressful to keep such sensitive, complex creatures inside an enclosed tank.

While SeaWorld initially countered that the filmmakers were guilty of giving false and misleading information, the fallout from the controversy was severe enough to cost one CEO's job and a thorough re-evaluation of the park's focus, which is now geared firmly toward its roller coasters and its animal encounters, with a strong emphasis on education and conservation. The much criticised 'One World' killer whale show has been replaced by the twice daily 'Orca Encounter,' where you learn about these animals rather than watch them do tricks.

SeaWorld's marine-themed, adrenaline-pumping roller coasters, however, brook no argument. **Kraken** is a whiplash zip of twists and turns in carriages with no floor so your feet dangle free. On **Manta** you lie horizontally, face down, several to a row, so that the coaster vaguely resembles a manta ray, and dive and fly through the air in this position, reaching speeds of almost 60mph. The newest ride, **Mako**, is the best of the three: replicating the high-speed twists and turns of a mako shark in full flow, the glass-smooth hyper coaster has a top speed of 73mph and features serious airtime as you 'float' over some of the bumps. There are also many attractions for the under 10s.

Pointe Orlando

Eating

Thai Thani
THAI $

7 ⊗ MAP P122, D5

A friendly, cool and quiet restaurant stuck out on its own in a mall (handy if you're staying near Sea-World), with gilded Thai decor and some tables with traditional floor seating. Good food, but if you want it spicy, ask for level 5 and above. (📞407-239-9733; www.thaithani.net; 11025 International Dr, International Dr; mains $14-24; ⊙11:30am-11pm; 🚼; 🚊I-Ride Trolley Red Line)

Slate
AMERICAN $$

8 ⊗ MAP P122, A2

One of Restaurant Row's brightest spots is this place that serves wood-fired meats and pizzas as well as seafood, light bites and on-point cocktails. The brain-child of Atlanta-based Concentrics, seating is divided between private and communal tables, as well as the wood room, a veranda-style space with a fireplace. (📞407-500-7528; www.slateorlando.com; 8323 W Sand Lake Rd, Restaurant Row; mains $21-42; ⊙4:30-10pm Mon-Fri, 11am-3pm & 4:30-11pm Sat, 11am-3pm & 4:30-9pm Sun)

Drinking

Icebar
BAR

9 🚇 MAP P122, C3

More classic Orlando gimmicky fun. Step into the 22°F (-5°C) ice house, sit on the ice seat, admire the ice carvings and sip the icy drinks. Jackets and gloves are provided at the door (or upgrade to the photogenic faux fur for $10), and the fire room, bathrooms and other areas of the bar are kept at normal temperature. (📞407-426-7555; www.icebarorlando.com; 8967 International Dr; entry at door/advance online $25/20; ⏰5pm-midnight Sun-Thu, to 2am Fri & Sat; 🚊I-Trolley Red Line Stop 18 or Green Line Stop 10)

Tin Roof
BAR, LIVE MUSIC

10 🚇 MAP P122, C2

The famous live-music joint that encourages performances of all standards. It's part of the I-Drive 360 complex (think the Wheel and more). Serves up reasonable (bordering on very nice) junk food – burgers, mac 'n' cheese – and things that will fuel you until the wee hours. (📞407-270-7926; www.tinroof orlando.com; 8371 International Dr, I-Drive 360, International Dr; ⏰noon-2am Mon-Fri, 11am-2am Sat & Sun)

Entertainment

Regal Pointe Orlando 4DX and IMAX
CINEMA

11 ⭐ MAP P122, C3

Multiplex cinema with a Screen X and IMAX screen as well as 4DX capability. (📞844-462-7342; www.regmovies.com; 9101 International Dr, International Dr; tickets adult/child from $13/10)

Shopping

Orlando Premium Outlets – Vineland Ave
MALL

12 🔒 MAP P122, A6

Popular outlet mall just outside Walt Disney World® – you'll know you're close when you're stuck in stand-still traffic for upwards of half an hour for no apparent reason. There's another **branch** (📞407-352-9600; www.premiumout lets.com/outlet/orlando-international; 4951 International Dr; ⏰10am-11pm Mon-Sat, to 9pm Sun; 🚌Lynx 8 or 42, 🚊I-Ride Trolley Red Line 1) just off International Dr. (📞407-238-7787; www.premiumoutlets.com/outlet/ orlando-vineland; 8200 Vineland Ave; ⏰10am-11pm Mon-Sat, to 9pm Sun; 🚊I-Ride Trolley Red Line 38)

Pointe Orlando
SHOPPING CENTER

13 🔒 MAP P122, C3

Pleasant enough, with brick walk-ways and a fountain, this small outdoor shopping area features an odd assortment of shops and several good restaurants. (📞407-248-2838; www.pointeorlandofl.com; 9101 International Dr; ⏰10am-10pm Mon-Sat, 11am-9pm Sun; 🚊I-Ride Trolley Red Line 18, 🚊I-Ride Trolley Green Line 11)

Downtown Orlando

Orlando has a lot to offer: lovely tree-lined neighborhoods, a rich performing arts and museum scene, several fantastic gardens and nature preserves, fabulous cuisine – and it's delightfully devoid of manic crowds. So come down off the coasters to explore the quieter, gentler side of the city. You may be surprised to find that you enjoy the theme parks all the more as a result.

The Short List

○ **Mennello Museum of American Art (p134)** *Everything in this small lakeside art museum is beautiful, including Earl Cunningham's work.*

○ **Leu Gardens (p134)** *Stunning array of flowers over 50 acres of landscaped garden.*

○ **Maxine's on Shine (p137)** *Fabulous neighborhood restaurant, bar and general hangout.*

○ **Mathers Social Gathering (p139)** *Elegant speakeasy-style bar on the 3rd floor of a 19th-century building in the heart of downtown.*

○ **Pig Floyd's Urban Barbakoa (p137)** *The tastiest barbecue in town has them lining up down the block.*

Getting There & Around

🚌 LYMMO circles downtown Orlando for free with stops near Lynx Central Station, near SunRail's Church St Station, at Central and Magnolia, Jefferson and Magnolia, and outside the Westin Grand Bohemian.

Neighbourhood Map on p132

Lake Eola Park (p135) JOHN COLETTI/GETTY IMAGES ©

Walking Tour 🚶

A Night Out in Downtown Orlando

Night is what downtown Orlando does best. Music filters out from the city's many bars, sidewalk tables invite lazy lingering over cocktails, and there's a rowdy college-town vibe as the night wears on. This local crawl takes you beyond the drink-pounding happy-hour specials into some of the city's best low-key favorites.

Walk Facts

Start DoveCote
End Mad Cow Theatre
Length 1 mile; 6 hours

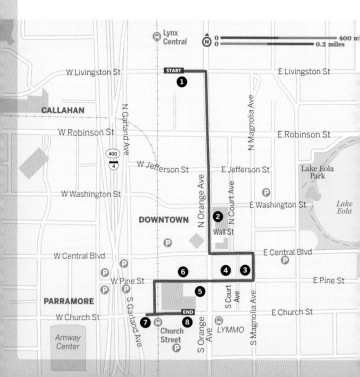

❶ Farm-to-Table Dinner

There's a festive vibe to dusk in downtown Orlando – music seeps out from pubs, business folk kick back over happy-hour beers, and outdoor bars bustle. It's important to start with some food, so head to DoveCote (p138) for some delicious French *cuisine paysanne* – the croque monsieur is highly recommended.

❷ Cocktails in the Woods

Get into the spirit of the night with a Vanishing Glass (or a Dinglehopper!) at the Woods (p141), located on the 2nd floor of the Historic Rose Building. With spirits from small-batch distilleries and an array of house-made syrups and infusions, this bar is noted for its unusual libations.

❸ Speakeasy Sophistication

Kick up the cocktail intake with a drink made just as they would have in the 1920s at Mathers Social Gathering (p139), located on the 3rd floor of a 19th-century building. This is one of the most beautiful bars in town.

❹ Additional Speakeasy Secrets

A password is required for entry into Hanson's Shoe Repair (p140), another intimate retreat that stylishly embraces the Prohibition-era speakeasy theme.

❺ Live Music

Take it up a notch at Tanqueray's (p142), an unpretentious underground haunt. It can get smoky and loud, but this little dive plays some of the best live local music in town.

❻ Halloween Mayhem

It's Halloween every night at Cocktails & Screams (p140), which welcomes freaks and Gothic geeks with a regular schedule of themed events. If you're here on a Wednesday, you'll be in the company of Addams Family look-alikes. You can escape into a secret 'coven bar', but you'll need to follow the clues on the walls to find the entrance.

❼ Late-Night Bites

Soak up some of that booze with a huge Hot Mess burger from Hamburger Mary's (p139) – available with a beef, chicken or veg-friendly blackbean patty. And don't forget a side order of sweet potato fries.

❽ Take in a Play

Too much carousing, not enough culture? Bypass the bars for a performance at the venerable Mad Cow Theatre (p141). This intimate regional playhouse regularly earns rave reviews for its stagings of local playwrights, theater classics such as *Cat on a Hot Tin Roof,* and Broadway hits.

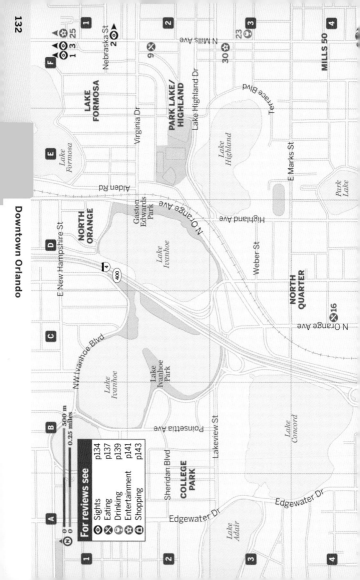

LAKE FORMOSA

LAKE FORMOSA

Nebraska St

PARK LAKE/ HIGHLAND

Lake Highland Dr

N Mills Ave

MILLS 50

Virginia Dr

Alden Rd

Lake Formosa

Lake Highland

Lake Highland Dr

Terrace Blvd

E Marks St

Park Lake

NORTH ORANGE

Gaston Edwards Park

Lake Ivanhoe

N Orange Ave

Highland Ave

Weber St

NORTH QUARTER

E New Hampshire St

400

NW Ivanhoe Blvd

Lake Ivanhoe

Lake Ivanhoe

Lake Ivanhoe Park

N Orange Ave

16

COLLEGE PARK

Poinsettia Ave

Lakeview St

Sheridan Blvd

Lakeview St

Lake Concord

Edgewater Dr

Edgewater Dr

Lake Adair

500 m
0.25 miles

For reviews see

Sights	p134
Eating	p137
Drinking	p139
Entertainment	p141
Shopping	p143

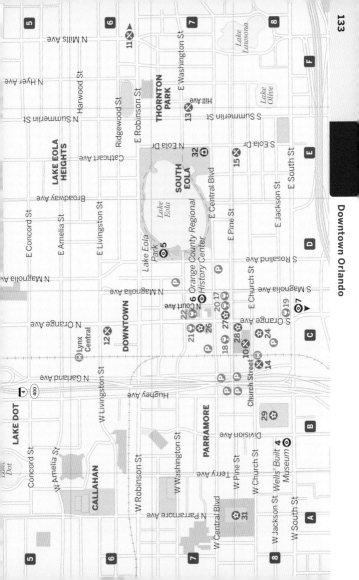

LAKE DOT

CALLAHAN

Lake Dot

Concord St

W Amelia St

W Robinson St

W Washington St

W Livingston St

N Garland Ave

Lynx Central

Hughey Ave

N Orange Ave

PARRAMORE

N Parramore Ave

W Central Blvd

Division Ave

Terry Ave

W Pine St

W Church St

W Jackson St

W South St

Wells' Built 4 Museum

31

29

DOWNTOWN

12

N Magnolia Ave

N Court Ave

22

6 Orange County Regional History Center

21

26

18

27 20 17

10 14

28

24

19 7

S Orange Ave

S Magnolia Ave

S Rosalind Ave

E Church St

E Jackson St

E South St

LAKE EOLA HEIGHTS

E Concord St

E Amelia St

E Livingston St

Broadway Ave

Cathcart Ave

Ridgewood St

E Robinson St

N Eola Dr

Lake Eola Park

Lake Eola

SOUTH EOLA

5

32

E Central Blvd

E Pine St

15

S Eola Dr

THORNTON PARK

13

Hill Ave

N Summerlin St

S Summerlin St

Lake Olive

Lake Lawsona

N Mills Ave

N Hyer Ave

11

Harwood St

Sights

Mennello Museum of American Art

MUSEUM

1 🎯 MAP P132, F1

Tiny but excellent lakeside art museum featuring the work of Earl Cunningham, whose brightly colored images, a fusion of pop and folk art, leap off the canvas. Visiting exhibits often feature American folk art. Every four months there's a new exhibition, everything from a Smithsonian collection to a local artist. The mystical live oak in front makes even parking beautiful. (📞407-246-4278; www.mennello museum.org; 900 E Princeton St, Loch Haven Park; adult/child 6-17yr $5/1; 🕙10:30am-4:30pm Tue-Sat, noon-4:30pm Sun; 🚌Lynx 125, 🚇Florida Hospital Health Village)

Leu Gardens

GARDENS

2 🎯 MAP P132, F1

Camellias, roses, orange groves and desert plants cover 50 acres, as well as plenty of grassy spots for a lakeside picnic. Pick up supplies at the trendy **East End Market** (📞231-236-3316; www.east endmkt.com; 3201 Corrine Dr, Audubon Park; 🕙8am-7pm Mon-Thu, to 9pm Fri & Sat, to 6pm Sun; 🅿️👫), a half-mile east of the entrance gate on Corrine Dr. Forty-five-minute tours of **Leu House**, a 19th-century mansion (later owned by the Leu family), run every half-hour from 10am to 1pm Tuesday to Sunday.

Earl Cunningham Gallery, Mennello Museum of American Art

See the website for details on outdoor movies, storytelling and ve music. (📞407-246-2620; www. eugardens.org; 1920 N Forest Ave, Loch Haven Park; adult/child 6-17yr $15/10; 🕒9am-5pm, last admission 4pm; 🚌Lynx 38, 8, 50)

Orlando Museum of Art
MUSEUM

◉ MAP P132, F1

Orlando's grand center for the arts is home to an impressive collection of mostly modern American artists. It hosts an array of adult and family-friendly art events and classes. The popular First Thursday ($15), from 6pm to 9pm on the first Thursday of the month, celebrates local artists with regional work, live music and food from Orlando restaurants.

The bulk of the permanent collection is made up of the work of the Florida Highwaymen, a group of 26 African American artists, including Alfred Hair, Harold Newton, AE Backus and Mary Ann Carroll, that between the 1950s and 1980s painted the underdeveloped Florida landscapes in a style of refined naturalism. They got their name because, as artists working outside the mainstream, they mostly sold their work by the side of the road. (📞407-896-4231; www.omart. org; 2416 N Mills Ave, Loch Haven Park, Downtown; adult/child $20/8; 🕒10am-4pm Tue-Fri, noon-4pm Sat & Sun; ♿; 🚌Lynx 125, 🚌Florida Hospital Health Village)

City Cycling

Though the streets of Orlando are not particularly bike-friendly, the city boasts a network of paved bike trails. Check out the website of local bike shop **Orange Cycle** (www. orangecycleorlando.com) for information and trail maps.

Wells' Built Museum
MUSEUM

4 ◉ MAP P132, B8

This small museum is dedicated to Orlando's African American history and culture. It's housed in the former Wells' Hotel, built in 1921 by Dr William Monroe Wells to host African American performers forbidden from staying in the city's strictly segregated accommodations. Through its doors passed many an influential performer, including Count Basie, Cab Calloway, Billie Holiday, Ella Fitzgerald and Duke Ellington. (📞407-245-7535; www.wellsbuilt. org; 511 W South St; adult/child $5/3; 🕒9am-5pm Mon-Fri)

Lake Eola Park
PARK

5 ◉ MAP P132, D7

Pretty and shaded, this little city park sits between downtown and Thornton Park. A paved sidewalk circles the water, there's a waterfront playground and you can rent swan paddleboats ($15 for 30 minutes). On Sunday mornings, the park is home to the Orlando Farmers Market (p143). (195 N Rosalind Ave; ⏲6am-midnight; ♿)

Orange County Regional History Center

MUSEUM

6 ⊙ MAP P132, C7

Orlando before Disney? Permanent exhibits cover prehistoric Florida, European exploration, race relations and citrus production, with a recreated pioneer home and 1927 courtroom. (☎407-836-8500; www.thehistorycenter.org; 65 E Centra Blvd, Downtown; adult/child 5-12yr $8/6; ⏲10am-5pm Mon-Sat, noon-5pm Sun; ♿)

Pulse Memorial

MEMORIA◀

7 ⊙ MAP P132, C8

Pending the construction of a permanent memorial for the victims of the June 12, 2016 shootings at the Pulse nightclub that left 49 people dead and 53 injured, this wall of photographs, testimonies and messages that surrounds the now shuttered building remains

Escape to Loch Haven Park

Just a couple of miles north of Downtown is picturesque Loch Haven Park, with 45 acres of parks, including the exquisite **Leu Gardens** (p134), and a handful of the city's best art museums: the **Orlando Museum of Art** (p135) and, especially, the **Mennello Museum of American Art** (p134). The nearby **Orlando Science Center** (☎407-514-2000; www.osc.org; 777 E Princeton St, Loch Haven Park; adult/child $24/18; ⏲10am-5pm; ♿; 🚌Lynx 125, 🚉Florida Hospital Health Village) is a great pitstop for young kids, with 3D movies, interactive displays, regularly changing exhibits, and (rather cute!) baby gators.

Start your exploration with a stick-to-your-bones breakfast and a Bloody Mary from **White Wolf Cafe** (☎407-895-9911; www.whitewolf cafe.com; 1829 N Orange Ave, Ivanhoe Village; mains $16-24; ⏲8am-3pm Sun-Wed, to 9pm Thu-Sat; 🚌Lynx 102) – then work it off with a wander through the park's gnarly oaks and dripping cypress (or just a snooze by the lake). You can also time your visit to coincide with a show at one of the city's best theater venues. Inside the park, the **John & Rita Lowndes Shakespeare Center** (☎407-447-1700; www.orlandoshakes.org; 812 E Rollins St, Loch Haven Park; tickets $15-65) hosts everything from *Beowulf* to *The Borrowers*, or the **Orlando Repertory Theater** (☎407-896-7365; www.orlandorep.com; 1001 E Princeton St, Loch Haven Park; tickets $12-30) features performances for families and children.

a moving tribute on behalf of the LGBTIQ+ and Latinx communities. (www.onepulsefoundation.org; 1912 S Orange Ave; ⏱7:30am-midnight)

Eating

Kabooki Sushi
SUSHI $

8 ⊗ MAP P132, F4

In an unassuming strip mall just east of Downtown is the best budget sushi spot in Orlando. Chef Henry Moso crafts nigiri, sashimi and makimono (sushi rolls) of such exquisite delicacy and flavor that the James Beard people saw fit to nominate him for a 2020 Rising Star Chef of the Year award. Best budget? Maybe just the best, period. (☎407-328-3839; www. kabookisushi.com; 3122 E Colonial Dr; mains $8-18; ⏱5-10pm Sun-Thu, to 11pm Fri & Sat)

Pig Floyd's Urban Barbakoa
BARBECUE $

9 ⊗ MAP P132, F2

A spin-off of the popular Tree-house food truck, this shack-style spot serves up sizzling Southern barbecue – brisket, ribs, pork belly and slaw. Throw in some Caribbean, Latin and Asian flavours (how about a Korean kimcheeze taco, or a crisp pork belly banh mi?) and you've got the best BBQ joint in town. The lines are worth it. (☎407-203-0866; https://pigfloyds. com; 1326 Mills Ave; mains $9-18; ⏱11am-9pm Tue-Thu & Sun, 11am-10pm Fri & Sat)

Mills 50 Dining
🍽

Dozens of Vietnamese, Korean, Chinese and other Asian eateries cluster along several blocks of Orlando's Mills 50 neighborhood, which has emerged in recent years as one of the best foodie spots in town.

Artisan's Table
AMERICAN $$

10 ⊗ MAP P132, C8

Chow down on the likes of a breakfast bowl of eggs and grits, or opt for steel-cut oats with agave and an organic smoothie at this under-the-radar locavore favorite offering an ever-changing and eclectic menu. There's even coffee and cocktails to start and end the day. If you want both, don't miss the cafe tequila, all fed through a fandangled gravity infusion tower. (☎407-730-7499; www.artisanstable orlando.com; 55 W Church St, Suite 128; mains $12-29; ⏱11am-9pm Wed-Sat, 11am-7pm Sun)

Maxine's on Shine
AMERICAN $$

11 ⊗ MAP P132, F6

This friendly bistro and retro bar is a firm neighborhood favorite. The mixed menu of European-infused dishes is tasty at any time, but the big draw is brunch. Chicken and waffles is the signature dish, while the Bloody Mary with a beer floater, bacon stir stick and shrimp cocktail garnish is almost a meal in itself. (📞407-674-6841; https://maxinesonshine.com; 337 N Shine Ave; mains brunch $12-17, dinner $14-27; 🕙brunch 10am-3pm Fri-Sun, dinner 5-9pm Thu-Sat)

DoveCote
FRENCH $$

12 ❌ MAP P132, C6

The decor – vivid blue, gold and other colors – is straight out of a Klimt painting, but this restaurant in the Bank of America building serves some mighty fine cuisine, best described as 'comfort French.' Sit in the brasserie and tuck into a delicious croque monsieur or a hot bowl of onion soup. There's also a coffee stop. (📞407-930-1700; www.dovecoteorlando.com; 390 N Orange Ave, Suite 110; mains lunch $11-29, dinner $18-32; 🕙11:30am-10pm Mon-Fri, 10:30am-2:30pm & 5:30-11pm Sat, 10:30am-2:30pm Sun)

Benjamin French Bakery
BAKERY $

13 ❌ MAP P132, F7

Rustic sandwiches, quiches and salads are lunchtime mainstays, but it's the pastries – especially those flavoured with chocolate by local chocolatier David Ramirez – that make this bright French bakery a treat. Sit at a sidewalk table and just let the day go by. (📞407-797-2293; www.benjaminfrenchbakery.com; 716 E Washington St, Thornton Park; pastries $4, mains $4-10; 🕙8am-3pm Mon-Fri, to 6pm Sat & Sun)

Reyes Mezcaleria

Hamburger Mary's
BURGERS $$

4 ✖ MAP P132, C8

Downtown high-energy diner specialising in over-the-top burgers with sweet-potato fries and serious cocktails. There's a Broadway Brunch with show tunes, Tuesday night drag shows and all kinds of interactive entertainment. (📞321-319-0600; www.hamburgermarys.com; 110 W Church St, Downtown; mains $12-18; ⏱11am-9pm Tue & Thu, 11am-4pm Wed & Sun 11am-10pm Fri & Sat)

Stubborn Mule
MODERN AMERICAN $$

5 ✖ MAP P132, E8

A trendy and very popular gastropub that serves handcrafted cocktails with flair (yes, plenty of mules) and good ol' locally sourced, delicious food that's nothing but contemporary – the likes of polenta cakes, smoked Gouda grits and roasted winter vegetables. Live music on weekends can make the outdoor seating a rather noisy affair. (www.thestubbornmuleorlando. com; 100 S Eola Dr, Suite 103, Downtown; mains $19-32; ⏱11am-10pm Mon-Thu, to 11pm Fri & Sat, to 9pm Sun)

Reyes Mezcaleria
MEXICAN $$

6 ✖ MAP P132, C4

This stylish, airy cantina-style Mexican joint in the heart of Downtown serves delicious tacos, empanadas and other Mexican

Orlando Bakeries 👍

Orlando's latest foodie trends include a wave of independently owned bakeries that specialise in decadent cupcakes, artisan pies and vegan delights. **P is for Pie** (📞407-745-4743; www.crazy forpies.com; 2806 Corrine Dr, Audubon Park; pies from $2.50; ⏱7:30am-2pm Tue-Sat) puts an artisan twist on classic pies – that is, sweet tarts with a biscuit base.

classics. There's a fine selection of wines, but ignore the margaritas and you're missing out on half the fun. (📞407-868-9007; www.reyes mex.com; 821 N Orange Ave; mains $15-24; ⏱11am-10pm Tue-Thu, to 11pm Fri & Sat, to 9pm Sun)

Drinking

Mathers Social Gathering
COCKTAIL BAR

17 🍸 MAP P132, C7

Our favorite bar in Orlando is on the 3rd floor of the 19th-century Mather Building, with a carefully designed speakeasy vibe and a killer menu of vintage, craft cocktails that are the best you'll have anywhere in town. Highly recommended. (www.mathers orlando.com; 30 S Magnolia Ave; ⏱4pm-2am Tue-Sat)

Wally's Mills Ave Liquors

Cocktails & Screams

COCKTAIL BAR

18 MAP P132, C7

It's Halloween year-round at this bar that opened in 2019 and quickly became an Orlando favorite – and not just with fans of all things horror and Gothic. It's part bar, part attraction in its own right and almost every night has themed events – Wednesday is Addams Family Night, so dress up! You'll scream, but mostly in delight.

Around the walls of the bar are clues that will eventually lead you to **Craft**, a 'secret coven bar' that serves even more potent potions and tinctures. (407-885-3558; https://cocktailsandscreams.com; 39

W Pine St; 7pm-2am Tue-Thu & Sat, to 5am Fri, to midnight Sun)

Bösendorfer Lounge

LOUNGE

19 MAP P132, C8

Zebra-fabric chairs, gilded mirrors, massive black pillars and marble floors ooze pomp and elegance. This hotel bar is popular for after-work drinks and the lounge picks up with live jazz at 7pm. The name comes from the lounge's rare Imperial Grand Bösendorfer piano, with its sculpted tree legs and music stand in the shape of a peacock with unfurled feathers. (407-313-9000; www.grandbohemianhotel. com; 325 S Orange Ave, Westin Grand Bohemian; midday-10pm)

Hanson's Shoe Repair

COCKTAIL BAR

20 MAP P132, C7

Orlando *loves* the Prohibition-era speakeasy theme, and this spot does it better than most, down to the historically accurate cocktails and a secret daily password for entry. Once inside, it's a cozy nest of folks having a quiet good time. Call or check its Twitter account (@hansonsshoeshop) for the password. There's a dress code – no sloppy gear. (407-476-9446; www.facebook.com/hansonsshoe repair; 3rd fl, 27 E Pine St, Downtown; 8pm-2am Tue-Thu & Sat, from 5pm Fri, from 3pm Sun)

Independent Bar

CLUB

21 🚇 MAP P132, C7

Half dive bar, half dance club, the 'I-Bar' squarely appeals to the non-EDM crowd with a menu of Top 40, old-school rock, '80s new wave and other popular retro genres. Hardly surprising that it promotes itself as the 'club for people who don't like clubs.' (📞407-839-0457; http://independentbar.net; 70 N Orange Ave, Downtown; cover varies; ⏱10pm-2:30am Sat-Thu, from 9:30pm Fri)

Woods

COCKTAIL BAR

22 🚇 MAP P132, C7

Craft cocktails and craft beers hidden in a cozy, smoke-free, 2nd-floor setting (in the historic Rose Building), with exposed brick, a tree-trunk bar and an earthy feel. (📞407-203-1114; www.thewoods orlando.com; 49 N Orange Ave, Downtown; ⏱5pm-2am Mon-Fri, 7pm-2am Sat, 4pm-midnight Sun)

Wally's Mills Ave Liquors

BAR

23 🚇 MAP P132, F3

It's been around since the early '50s, before Orlando became Disney, and while its peeling, naked-women wallpaper could use some updating, it wouldn't be Wally's without it. Nothing flashy, nothing loud, just a tiny, window-less, smoky bar with a jukebox and cheap, strong drinks – as much a dark dive as you'll find anywhere.

Wednesday night is $3 micro-brews, Monday is $2 PBR beer, and the attached package store sells beer, wine and liquor. (📞407-896-6975; www.wallysbarandliquors.com; 1001 N Mills Ave, Thornton Park; ⏱7am-2am Mon-Sat, 9am-2am Sun)

Entertainment

Mad Cow Theatre

THEATER

24 ⭐ MAP P132, C8

A model of inspiring regional theater, with classic and modern performances in a Downtown Orlando space (located on the 2nd floor). (📞407-297-8788; www.madcowtheatre.com; 54 W Church St, Downtown; tickets from $30)

Festivals & Events

Walt Disney World® and Universal Orlando Resort celebrate the holidays with seasonal shows and parades. In addition, Orlando hosts an excellent Fringe Festival (along the lines of the Edinburgh Festival); a film festival; the Zora! Festival, celebrating author Zora Neale Hurston; the GayDays festival; and the quirky Megacon, a huge comic sci-fi, horror, anime and gaming event. The website of the official tourism body, Visit Orlando, has a good month-by-month listing of what's on (www.visitorlando.com/events).

Enzian Theater
CINEMA

25 ⭐ MAP P132, F1

'Film is Art' is the slogan of this clapboard-sided theater that could be the envy of any college town. Independent and classic films are the mainstay, while the excellent **Eden Bar** (📞 407-629-1088; mains $9-12; 🕐 11am-11pm Sun-Thu, to 1am Fri & Sat; 🖋) restaurant has primarily local and organic fare. Have a veggie burger and a beer on the patio underneath the cypress tree or opt for table service in the theater. (📞 407-629-0054; www. enzian.org; 1300 S Orlando Ave, Maitland; adult/child $12/10; 🕐 5pm-midnight Tue-Fri, noon-midnight Sat & Sun)

Beacham & the Social
LIVE MUSIC

26 ⭐ MAP P132, C7

Both the Beacham and the more intimate and recommended Social next door are cornerstones of Orlando's nightclub and live-music scene. They host bands from punk to reggae on the weekends and hop all week long with music and dancing. Shows are designated 'all ages,' '18 plus' or '21 plus.' (📞 407-246-1419; www. thebeacham.com; 46 N Orange Ave, Downtown; 🕐 9pm-3am)

SAK Comedy Lab
COMEDY

27 ⭐ MAP P132, C7

Excellent improv comedy in an intimate downtown Orlando theater. It's on the 2nd floor of the City Arts Factory. (📞 407-648-0001; www.sakcomedylab.com; 29 S Orange Ave, Downtown; tickets $20, 9pm Tue & Wed $7; 🕐 Tue-Sat)

Tanqueray's Downtown Orlando
LIVE MUSIC

28 ⭐ MAP P132, C8

A former bank vault, this underground smoky dive bar draws folks looking to hang out with friends over a beer. There's Guinness on tap, and you can catch local bands usually reggae or blues, on the weekend. (📞 407-649-8540; 100 S Orange Ave, Downtown; 🕐 5pm-2am Mon-Fri, 8pm-2am Sat & Sun)

Amway Center
SPECTATOR SPORT

29 ⭐ MAP P132, B8

The Orlando Magic (National Basketball Association), the Orlando Predators (Arena Football League) and the Orlando Solar Bears (East Coast Hockey League) play here. (📞 407-440-7000; www. amwaycenter.com; 400 W Church St, Downtown)

Will's Pub
LIVE MUSIC

30 ⭐ MAP P132, F3

With $3 Pabst on tap, pinball, and vintage pin-ups on the walls, this is Orlando's less-polished music scene, but it enjoys a solid reputation as one of the best spots in town to catch local and nationally touring indie music. Smoke-free; beer and wine only. (📞 407-898-5070; www.willspub.org; 1042 N Mills Ave, Thornton Park; tickets $10-20; 🕐 4pm-2am Mon-Sat, from 6pm Sun)

Exploria Stadium

Exploria Stadium

SPECTATOR SPORT

31 ⭐ MAP P132, A8

This 25,000-seat stadium in the heart of Downtown is the home of Major League Soccer team Orlando City FC and Orlando Pride of the National Women's Soccer League. (www.orlandocitysc.com; 655 W Church St; tickets from $31; ⊙mid-Feb–Oct)

Shopping

Orlando Farmers Market

MARKET

32 🔒 MAP P132, E7

Local produce and a beer and wine garden on the shores of downtown Orlando's Lake Eola. (www.orlandofarmersmarket.com; Lake Eola; ⊙10am-3pm Sun)

Worth a Trip 🔭
Learn about Rocket Launches at the Kennedy Space Center

One of Florida's most visited attractions, this 140,000-acre site was once the US' primary space-flight facility, where shuttles were built and astronauts rocketed into the cosmos. Although NASA indefinitely terminated its shuttle program in 2011, shifting the center from a living museum to a historical one, new plans are afoot to send astronauts to the moon, Mars and beyond.

📞 855-433-4210

kennedyspacecenter.com

NASA Pkwy, State Rd 405, Merritt Island

adult/child 3-11yr $75/65

🕙 10am-4pm, to 8pm for special events

Kennedy Space Center Bus Tour

This 90-minute bus tour is the only way to see beyond the Visitor Complex without paying for an add-on tour. The first stop is the **LC 39 Observation Gantry**, a 60ft observation tower with views of the twin launch pads. From here, the bus winds through the launch facilities to the **Apollo/Saturn V Center**, where you don't want to miss the multimedia show in the Firing Room. Video footage on three screens depicts America's first lunar mission, the 1968 launch of *Apollo VIII*, before you're ushered through to an enormous hangar displaying the real *Apollo 14* Command Module and the 363ft, 6.5-million-lb *Saturn V* moon rocket.

Tours depart every 15 minutes from 10am to 3:30pm. Look for the coach buses and long lines to the right when you enter the Visitor Complex.

Space Shuttle Atlantis

Blasted by rocket fuel and streaked with space dust, space shuttle *Atlantis,* the final orbiter among NASA's fleet, is the most impressive exhibit in the complex. Suspended in a specially designed, $100-million space, it hangs just a few feet out of reach, nose down, payload doors open, as if it's still orbiting the earth. It's a creative and dramatic display, preceded by a chest-swelling film that tells the story of the shuttle program from its inception in the 1960s to *Atlantis'* final mission in 2011.

Around the shuttle, interactive consoles invite visitors to try to land it or dock it to the International Space Station, touchscreens offer details of missions and crews, and there's a full-size replica of the Hubble Space Telescope and a not-very-scary 'shuttle launch experience.' Docents, many of whom worked on the shuttle program, are stationed around the exhibits to answer questions and tell tall space tales.

★ **Top Tips**

• Add-on tours must be reserved in advance.

• Time your visit to coincide with a crewless rocket or satellite launch; visit www.spacecoast launches.com for the schedule.

• Bring valid ID; non-US nationals will need a passport.

✕ **Take a Break**

Eat freshly caught sustainable goodies at **Wild Ocean Seafood** (www. wildoceanmarket.com; 688 S Park Ave; mains $9-12; ⏱11am-6pm Wed & Thu, 10am-6pm Fri & Sat, 11am-4pm Sun) market. Head across the causeway, 7 miles north on Hwy 1 and west on South St.

★ **Getting There**

🚌 Gray Line offers round-trip transportation from Orlando locations ($79).

🚗 The Space Center is east across the NASA Pkwy on SR 405. Parking costs $10.

Heroes & Legends and the US Astronaut Hall of Fame

Next to the Rocket Garden, the newest exhibit at the center celebrates pioneers of NASA's early space programs, inspiring a new generation to keep their intergalactic dreams alive. It starts with a 360-degree film on the lives of astronauts, then guides visitors through displays of a Redstone rocket, space shuttles and astronauts' personal belongings, along with stations organized under character traits of astronauts, such as 'passionate,' 'tenacious' and 'disciplined.'

The exhibit also features the Mercury Mission Control room and the 4D movie *Through the Eyes of a Hero,* about the lives of the 93 Hall of Fame inductees. Finally, inside the relocated and revamped US Astronaut Hall of Fame, visitors are welcomed by a statue of Alan Shepard, along with interactive video displays of the astronauts and their missions.

Rocket Garden

Wander among real and replica rocket capsules that launched the American Space Program. You can climb into some of them – it's amazing to see how tiny the cockpits are, and to imagine real astronauts sitting exactly where you are sitting. But instead of sipping on that giant Dr Pepper in the Florida sun, they were shooting up through the atmosphere. Little ones can cool off in the spurting fountain on the far corner of Rocket Garden.

Meet an Astronaut

You can meet an astronaut at the **Astronaut Encounter**, held daily inside the Astronaut Encounter Theater and included in park admission. Don't confuse this with the Mission Status Briefing, which is held in the same theater. Check your park map for times. Alternatively, **Chat with an Astronaut** (adult/child $50/35) is a morning-tea or afternoon-tea lecture followed by a Q&A. Register in advance online or check same-day availability at the Ticket Plaza upon entering the park.

Space Mirror Memorial

The stunningly beautiful Space Mirror Memorial, a shiny granite wall standing four stories high, reflects both literally and figuratively on the personal and tragic stories behind the theme-park energy that permeates the center. Several stone panels display the photos and names of those who died in space disasters.

IMAX Theater

Within the Visitor Complex, an IMAX theater shows two delightful films that include clear explanations of complicated science and footage shot from space. A Beautiful Planet, narrated by Jennifer Lawrence, offers a look at the effect of humans on planet Earth and an optimistic take on the future, and Journey to Space 3D features interviews with astronauts and an exciting overview of NASA's past, present and future undertakings.

Add-on Experiences

Extended tours offer the opportunity to visit the **Vehicle Assembly Building**, **Cape Canaveral Air Force Station** and its launch sites, and the **Launch Control Center**, where engineers perform system checks. The **Astronaut Training Experience** simulates what life on Mars might be like, while the **Cosmic Quest** is an action-oriented game-play experience featuring real NASA missions involving rocket launch, redirection of an asteroid and building a Martian habitat.

Worth a Trip 👀
See the Wonders Built from Bricks at Legoland® Florida Resort

Legoland is a joy. With manageable crowds and lines, this lakeside theme park maintains an old-school vibe – you don't have to plan like a general, and it's strikingly stress-free and relaxed. This is about fun (and yes, education) in a colorful and interactive environment. Rides and attractions, including the attached water park, are geared toward children aged two to 12.

📞 863-318-5346

www.legoland.com/florida

1 Legoland Way

tickets 1-/2-day $100/125, child under 2yr free

🕙 10am-5pm, sometimes later

Rides & Shows

There's plenty for little ones to love, including a foam ball play area, splash fountains and kiddie rides. At **Ford Driving School**, tiny tots can drive cars through a pretend town and earn an official license, and the lakeside water-ski show is pure silly pirate fun. The park's roller coaster thrills are the **Great Lego Race**, the **Dragon**, **Coastersaurus** (the park's classic wooden coaster), plus **Flying School**, a coaster that zips you around with your feet dangling free. The water park offers high-speed slides and a lazy river. Kids love **Mia's Riding Adventure**, a horse-themed 'disc' coaster.

Miniland USA

Anyone who has ever tried to build with Lego bricks will be wowed by the intricate designs and painstaking detail of these Lego models of iconic American cities and scenes from *Star Wars* films. Though amazingly accurate, there's a sense of humor here, such as the interactive water and sound features. Oh, and keep an eye out for whimsical scenarios such as the crazy cat lady.

Ninjago

As well as meeting characters like Kai, Legoland's martial-art-themed area includes an interactive ride where you can score points using up to five different ninja hand maneuvers to zap fireballs, lightning and the like (as seen through your 4D glasses, of course). It's remarkable technology and, oh, such fun.

Imagination Zone

Don't miss this wonderful indoor space. This colorful, interactive learning center has themed zones, and skilled Lego makers are on hand to help children of all ages create something from the thousands of Lego bricks.

★ Top Tips

o Save money by buying entry tickets at least two days ahead.

o If you're with little'uns under two years old, take advantage of the 'tot spots' with Duplo, among other things.

o Winter Haven's collection of restaurants in sleepy downtown are worth exploring.

✕ Take a Break

Stop by the retro-dive **Donut Man** (☎863-293-4031, 863-514-7727; 1290 6th St; doughnuts from $1.50; ⏰5:30am-10pm; 🚻) for doughnuts on the way to Legoland. For lunch in the park, pick up a sandwich from Lakeside Sandwich Co.

★ Getting There

The Legoland Shuttle ($5) runs daily from I-Drive 360 (near the Wheel at Icon Park). Park on the bottom floor of the I-Drive 360 parking lot (free).

Worth a Trip 🔭
Escape to Elegant Winter Park

Orlandoans are justifiably proud of bucolic Winter Park, which may be a city in its own right but is very much a part of the Orlando experience. Just north of Downtown, it's home to a handful of excellent museums and some of the most talked-about restaurants in all of Greater Orlando – all within a few shaded, pedestrian-friendly streets.

From downtown Orlando, take I-4 to Fairbanks Ave and head east for about 2 miles to Park Ave. Orlando's SunRail and Lynx 102 services stop at Winter Park.

Charles Hosmer Morse Museum of American Art

Internationally famous, the stunning and delightful **Charles Hosmer Morse Museum of American Art** (📞 407-645-5311; www.morse museum.org; 445 N Park Ave; adult/child $6/1, 4-8pm Fri Nov-Apr free; ⏱9:30am-4pm Tue-Sat, 1-4pm Sun) houses the world's most comprehensive collection of Louis Comfort Tiffany art. Highlights include the chapel interior designed by the artist for the 1893 World's Columbian Exhibition in Chicago; 10 galleries filled with architectural and art objects from Tiffany's Long Island home, Laurelton Hall; and an installation of the Laurelton's Daffodil Terrace.

More Museums

Winter Park's rep as a haven of high culture is enhanced by a handful of smaller museums. The **Cornell Fine Arts Museum** (pictured; www.rollins. edu/cfam; Rollins College, 1000 Holt Ave; admission free; ⏱10am-7pm Tue, to 4pm Wed-Fri, noon-5pm Sat & Sun), on the Rollins College campus, has over 700 paintings from the 14th century to today, including some exquisite European Old Masters. At the **Hannibal Square Heritage Center** (📞 407-539-2680; www.hannibalsquare heritagecenter.org; 642 W New England Ave; admission free; ⏱noon-4pm Tue-Fri, 10am-2pm Sat), the history of Winter Park's African American community (mostly locally employed laborers, carpenters and farmers) is told through photographs and poignant oral history. And you don't have to be a fan of Czech sculptor Albin Polasek to enjoy his former **home** (www.polasek.org; 633 Osceola Ave; adult/child $12/7; ⏱10am-4pm Tue-Sat, 1-4pm Sun), now a museum of his work and listed on the National Register of Historic Places.

★ **Top Tips**

o The Charles Hosmer Morse museum offers first-come, first-serve tours of Laurelton Hall at 2:30pm Tuesday and Thursday.

o March sees the **Winter Park Sidewalk Art Festival** (📞 407-644-7207; www.wpsaf.org; Winter Park; ⏱Mar), the oldest of its kind in Florida.

✕ **Take a Break**

The **Wine Room** (📞 407-696-9463; www.thewineroom online.com; 270 S Park Ave; tastings from $4; ⏱2pm-midnight Mon-Thu, 11am-12:30am Fri & Sat, noon-11pm Sun) offers more than 150 wines in 1oz, 2.5oz or 5oz pours.

Scenic Boat Tour

One of the best ways to appreciate the under-the-radar beauty and classic Florida escape of Winter Park is to meander over to Lake Osceola for a one-hour boat tour with **Scenic Boat Tour** (📞407-644-4056; www. scenicboattours.com; 312 E Morse Blvd; adult/child $16/8; ⏰hourly 10am-4pm; 👪). Hop on an 18-passenger pontoon and cruise through tropical canals, past mansions, Rollins College and other sights. You'll learn much about the area's history and gossip about the houses on the lake – and you might also spot a sleeping alligator or a crane looking to feed in the water.

If you'd rather explore on your own, the company also rents canoes and rowboats.

Winter Park Dining

Some of Orlando's best farm-to-table restaurants are in Winter Park, which means there's no shortage of discerning Orlandoans rolling in for a good meal. **Prato** (📞407-262-0050; www.prato-wp.com; 124 N Park Ave; mains $17-20; ⏰5:30-10pm Mon & Tue, 11:30am-11pm Wed-Sat, to 10pm Sun) does high-quality Italian (the pizzas are particularly good), while at **Ravenous Pig** (📞407-628-2333; www.theravenouspig.com; 565 W Fairbanks Ave; mains $18-40; ⏰4-10pm Tue-Thu, to 11pm Fri, 11am-11pm Sat, to 10pm Sun), Orlando's love affair with gourmet Southern BBQ is given full expression. For exclusively plant-based cuisine, you'll have to go far to find a place better than **Ethos Vegan Kitchen** (📞407-228-3898;

Winter Park Farmers' Market

ww.ethosvegankitchen.com; 601b S
Iew York Ave; mains $10-17; ⏰9am-
1pm; 🍴) on New York Ave.

If you're looking for all-day
breakfast, the much-loved **Keke's
Breakfast Cafe** (📞407-629-1400;
vww.kekes.com; 345 W Fairbanks Ave;
mains $10-15; ⏰7am-2:30pm; 🍴) is
part of a Florida chain and has a
pleasant branch in Winter Park.

Alfond Inn

Even if you don't stay here, you
should explore the lobby spaces
of this superb boutique **hotel**
(📞407-998-8090; www.thealfondinn.
com; 300 E New England Ave; r from
$300; ❄@📶🏊🐾). Contem-
porary white-walled elegance,
a low-key welcoming vibe, and
colorful interiors in well-appointed
rooms give this Winter Park gem
a distinct style. The hotel has a
strong commitment to the arts:
not only does it house the **Alfond
Collection of Contemporary
Art**, part of the Cornell Fine Arts
Museum's permanent collection,
but all profits fund liberal-arts
scholarships at Rollins College.
There's a lovely rooftop pool and
an excellent restaurant that serves
locally sourced food on courtyard
tables.

Winter Park
Farmers' Market

Winter Park's historic train
station, with its original brick
walls and massive vintage
wooden sliding doors, houses
the Saturday morning **Winter
Park Farmers' Market** (200 W
New England Ave; ⏰8am-1pm Sat).
You'll find local cheeses and
honey, flowers and herbs, along
with several excellent stands
selling baked goods, spread
out in the station and through
the gardens.

It's a small market, but a
lovely spot to people-watch over
a cup of coffee or an organic
Popsicle.

Shopping

Head to Winter Park for pleasant
browsing, small-town American
style. You can shop for beautiful
stationery at the **Rifle Paper Co**
(📞407-622-7679; www.riflepaper
co.com; 558 W New England Ave;
⏰10am-5pm Mon-Sat) and, if you've
got a sweet tooth, make sure to
stop by **Rocket Fizz** (📞407-645-
3499; www.rocketfizz.com; 520 S Park
Ave; ⏰10am-9pm Mon-Wed, to 11pm
Thu-Sat, 11am-6pm Sun).

Survival Guide

Before You Go

Book Your Stay

○ All Disney and Universal hotels (on site) offer free transfers to and from their respective parks, which can lead to substantial savings.

○ Disney doesn't guarantee connecting rooms unless your party has more children than adults.

○ Off-site hotels often include some kind of breakfast in their rates; on-site hotels never do.

○ You've a better chance of receiving one of Disney's exclusive 'PIN code' offers if your name, address and email are in its system.

Useful Websites

Lonely Planet (www.lonelyplanet.com) Writer-recommended reviews and online booking.

ReserveOrlando (www.reserveorlando.com) Central booking agency.

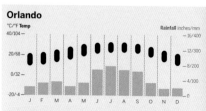

When to Go

○ **Winter** (Dec–Feb) Christmas through early January draws massive theme-park crowds. Otherwise, low-season bargains abound as temps can dip below freezing.

○ **Spring** (Mar–May) March to April is peak tourism season thanks to spring breakers. Crowds thin in May.

○ **Summer** (Jun–Aug) Busy with summer holiday crowds, lots of festivals. Hot and humid; 90-degree-plus temperatures.

○ **Autumn** (Sep–Nov) The masses diminish after Labor Day, except for Halloween festivities. Lodging prices plummet and summer sizzle fades.

Orlando Visitors Center (www.visitorlando.com) Options from the tourism office's jam-packed website.

Orlando Vacation Home Rental (www.orlando-vacationhomerental.com) Predominantly gated community homes.

Universal Orlando Resort (www.universalorlando.com) On-site hotels at Universal Orlando Resort.

DIS (www.wdwinfo.com) Loads of details and photos of Walt Disney World® and Lake Buena Vista hotels.

Best Budget

○ **Disney's Fort Wilderness Resort** (www.disneyworld.com) Cabins and campground in a natural preserve. Has nightly campfire sing-alongs.

○ **Floridian Hotel & Suites** (www.floridianhotelorlando.com) This

Walt Disney World® Resort Hotels

Disney resort hotels are divided according to location (Magic King-dom, Epcot, Animal Kingdom and Disney's BoardWalk). Prices vary drastically according to season, week and day.

Disney's website (www.disneyworld.com) outlines all its resorts and package offerings. Most rooms sleep up to four, with no extra charge for children or cribs, and a handful offer themed rooms and bunk beds.

While deluxe resorts are the best Disney has to offer, note that you're paying for Disney theming and location convenience, not luxury. Most offer multiroom suites and villas, upscale restaurants, children's programs and easy access to theme parks. Epcot resorts offer walking access and pleasant boat transport to restaurants and entertainment at Disney's BoardWalk, Hollywood Studios and Epcot, while Magic Kingdom resorts are an easy boat or monorail ride to park gates.

Five value resorts, the least-expensive Disney properties available (not including camping), have thousands of motel-style rooms and suites; are garishly decorated according to their theme; connect to all the parks by bus only; and cater to families and traveling school groups – expect cheerleader teams practicing in the courtyard or a lobby of teenagers wearing matching jerseys. You will definitely feel the difference because of the lower price: instead of proper restaurants, there are food courts and snack bars, and things are particularly bright, hectic and loud. Some value resorts offer family suites with two bathrooms and a kitchenette.

Staying Around Walt Disney World®

If you don't stay in a Walt Disney World® resort, countless other hotels, motels and resorts in Lake Buena Vista, Kissimmee and Celebration lie within a few miles of Walt Disney World®. There's an excellent selection of chain motels along grassy Palm Pkwy just out-side Disney's gates and a cluster of seven upscale chain hotels (www.downtowndisneyhotels.com) across from Disney Springs.

wonderful, privately owned hotel has spot-less rooms and compli-mentary breakfast.

○ **Universal's Endless Summer Resort** (www.universalorlando.com) Two on-site hotels – Dockside and Surfside – that echo California's easy, breezy '60s surf culture.

○ **Disney's Pop Century Resort** (www.disney world.com) Bright, cheer-ful hotel that pays tribute to the different decades of the 20th century.

Universal Orlando Resort Hotels

Universal Orlando Resort has eight excellent resort hotels divided into four pricing categories: value, prime value, preferred and premier. The bulk of its hotels are themed to evoke a summery vibe of yesteryear, and for the most part they work. Staying at a resort eliminates many logistical hassles: it's a pleasant gardened walk or a quiet boat ride to the parks; most offer Unlimited Express Pass access to park attractions and priority dining; several popular rides, such as the Wizarding World of Harry Potter, open one hour early for all guests; and the Loews Loves Pets program welcomes Fido as a VIP.

Best Midrange

○ **Hyatt Regency Grand Cypress Resort** (www.hyattregencygrandcypress.com) Quality rooms, service, grounds and amenities, 7 miles from Disney's Magic Kingdom.

○ **Walt Disney World® Swan & Dolphin Resort** (www.swandolphin.com) Two high-rise luxury hotels with a distinctly toned-down Disney feel but all the Disney perks.

○ **Hilton Orlando Bonnet Creek** (www.hiltonbonnetcreek.com) Big pool with lazy river, and surrounded by Walt Disney World® Resort, but without the mayhem.

○ **Cabana Bay Beach Resort** (www.universalorlando.com) Family suites themed like a colorful 1950s motel.

○ **Disney's Coronado Springs Resort** (www.disneyworld.com) Southwestern theme with a low-key tone that sets it apart from other Disney hotels.

Best Top End

○ **Disney's BoardWalk Inn** (www.disneyworld.com) Elegantly evokes the seaside charm of 1930s Atlantic City.

○ **Bay Hill Club & Lodge** (www.bayhill.com) Reassuringly calm and simple. Gracious staff and handsome rooms.

○ **Disney's Animal Kingdom Lodge** (www.disneyworld.com) Elegant, African savanna–themed hotel with plenty of wildlife in the grounds.

○ **Four Seasons Resort Orlando at Walt Disney World®** (www.fourseasons.com) All the luxury and attention to detail you'd expect from a Four Seasons resort.

○ **Alfond Inn** (www.thealfondinn.com) Boutique hotel with a welcoming vibe in Winter Park.

○ **Disney's Grand Floridian Resort & Spa** (www.disneyworld.com) The grandest Disney property of all.

Arriving in Orlando

Orlando International Airport

○ **Disney's Magical Express** (☎866-599-0951; www.disneyworld.com) Complimentary coach transfer from Orlando International Airport to Walt Disney World® resorts (book in advance).

○ **Orlando Airport Towncar** (☎800-532-8563; www.orlandoairporttowncar.com) Transport to Walt Disney World® costs one way/return $60/120 for one to four people in a town car; $85/170 for one to six people in an SUV. It's about the same cost for transport to Universal Orlando Resort or other hotels. Meet at baggage claim.

○ **Legacy Towncar of Orlando** (☎888-939-8227; www.legacytowncar.com) Round-trip to Universal, Walt Disney World® or International Drive costs $135 for a town car seating up to four people; $160 for a five- to nine-person van. Prices include a 20-minute grocery-store stop.

○ **Lynx** (☎407-841-2279, route info 407-841-8240; www.golynx.com; 455 Garland Ave, Downtown; per ride/day/week $2/4.50/16, transfers free; ⏰call center 8am-8pm Mon-Fri, 8am-6pm Sat & Sun) Located in Terminal A. Bus 42 to International Drive takes one hour.

○ **Taxi** Rides to Lake Buena Vista and Universal Orlando Resort area take 25 to 35 minutes (depending on traffic) and cost $55 to $70.

Orlando Sanford International Airport

○ **Town car** Both Orlando Airport Towncar and Legacy Towncar of Orlando provide transport to destinations including Lake Buena Vista for around $100/175 return. Meet at baggage claim.

○ **Taxi** Rides to Lake Buena Vista take an hour and cost $120 to $130; to the Universal Orlando Resort area, it costs $85 to $100 and takes about 40 minutes.

Getting Around

Disney Transportation

○ Both Walt Disney World® Resort and Universal Orlando Resort operate free boat and bus links between their respective parks, hotels and entertainment districts.

○ Disney has three monorail routes connecting Magic Kingdom, Epcot, select hotels and the **Transportation & Ticket Center** (www.disneyworld.com; Walt Disney World®; Magic Kingdom parking $25).

○ Allow at least one hour to get from point A to B, especially within Walt Disney World®.

○ There's no Disney transportation from Disney Springs to the parks.

○ Free parking is available for dinner reservations at Disney's Polynesian, Grand Floridian and Contemporary Resorts.

○ Be prepared for very long lines at the Transportation & Ticket Center during busy times.

Universal Orlando Resort Transportation

○ Boats connect City-Walk and theme parks to deluxe resorts; they run from one hour before early admission to Wizarding World of Harry Potter to 2:30am.

○ To get to the theme parks from Cabana Bay,

Getting Around Universal Orlando Resort

Universal Orlando Resort – that is, Universal Orlando's resort hotels, Islands of Adventure and Universal Studios theme parks and the shopping, dining and entertainment center at CityWalk – are linked by pedestrian walkways. It's a 10- to 15-minute walk from the theme parks and CityWalk to the deluxe resort hotels. Cabana Bay Beach Resort is about a 25-minute walk. Several hotels outside the park are within a 20-minute walk, but it's not a very pleasant journey.

you must take a five-minute shuttle to the transportation hub, and then walk 10 minutes through CityWalk.

Bus

o **LYMMO** (www.golynx. com; free; ☉6am-10:45pm Mon-Fri, from 10am Sat, 10am-10pm Sun) circles downtown Orlando for free with stops near Lynx Central Station, near SunRail's Church St Station, at Central and Magnolia, Jefferson and Magnolia and outside the Westin Grand Bohemian.

Car & Motorcycle

o Both Orlando International and Orlando Sanford International Airports, Walt Disney World® and many hotels have car-rental agencies.

o Disney's **Car Care Center** (Map p40, C3; ☎407-824-3470; www. disneyworld.com; 1000 Car Care Dr; ☉7am-7pm Mon-Fri, to 4pm Sat, to 3pm Sun) and the Walt Disney World® Dolphin Hotel offer Alamo and National car rentals, and there are rental-car desks at Universal Orlando Resort Hotels.

I-Ride Trolley

o The **I-Ride Trolley** (☎407-354-5656; www. iridetrolley.com; rides adult/child 3-9yr $2/1, passes 1/3/5/7/14 days $5/7/9/12/18; ☉8am-10:30pm) runs virtually the whole length of International Drive

o Buy one-day ($5) and multiday (from $7 for three days) tickets at hotels and sights along International Drive.

o Only exact fare, in cash, is accepted on board ($2).

o To get to Universal Orlando Resort, get off at Universal's Volcano Bay and walk 15 minutes over the interstate.

Shuttle

o Call **Mears Transportation** (☎855-463-2776; www.mearstransportation. com) one day in advance to arrange personalized transport between a long list of hotels and many attractions, including Universal Orlando Resort, SeaWorld and Busch Gardens. It costs between $25 and $35 per round-trip per person.

o **Casablanca Transportation** (☎407-927-2773; www.casablanca transportation.com) provides good service to the airport and in and around Orlando.

Taxi

❍ Cabs sit outside the theme parks, Disney Springs, resorts and other tourist centers.

❍ If taking a taxi to Magic Kingdom, ask to be dropped off at the Contemporary Resort; from here, it is an easy five-minute walk to the gates of Magic Kingdom. Otherwise, they drop you off at the Transportation & Ticket Center and you must take a ferry or monorail to the park.

❍ Ride-share services like Uber and Lyft are usually much cheaper than taxis.

SunRail

❍ North–south running commuter **rail** (www. sunrail.com) runs Monday to Friday.

❍ Convenient stops include Winter Park (downtown Winter Park), Florida Hospital Health Village (Loch Haven Park) and Church St (downtown Orlando).

❍ Tickets range in price from $2 to $7.50.

Essential Information

Accessible Travel

❍ Accommodations in Florida are required by law to offer wheelchair-accessible rooms. For questions about specialty rooms at Walt Disney World® Resort call ☎ 407-939-7807.

❍ Parks allow guests with special needs to avoid waiting in line, but do not offer front-of-the-line access. Disney issues a Disability Access Service card and Universal Orlando Resort issues the Attraction Assistance Pass (AAP). Guests take the card to the attraction they want to experience and they are given a return time based on current wait times. Both are available at Guest Services inside the park.

❍ Wheelchair and electric convenience vehicle (ECV) rental is available at Guest Services at Walt Disney World® Resort, Universal Orlando Resort and SeaWorld.

❍ Go to individual park websites or Guest Services for details on accessibility, services for guests with cognitive disabilities, services for guests who are deaf or have hearing

Lockers

Lots of rides throughout the parks require that all loose items, including backpacks and small purses, be secured in complimentary short-term lockers conveniently located at the ride entrance. Both Walt Disney World® and Universal Orlando Resort, however, also have all-day lockers of various sizes starting at $10 per day, which are especially useful if you're in a water park or don't want to carry everything around with you all the time.

You can pay with credit card, or use a MagicBand at Disney and TapuTapu at Universal's Volcano Bay.

Walt Disney World® Resort Tickets

Multiday tickets Valid for one theme park per day for each day of the ticket (you can leave/re-enter the park but cannot enter another park).

Park Hopper Gives same-day admission to any/all of the four Walt Disney World® parks. Fair warning: hopping between four parks requires a lot of stamina. Two parks a day is more feasible.

Park Hopper Plus The same as Park Hopper, but you can toss in Blizzard Beach, Typhoon Lagoon and Oak Trail Golf Course. The number of places you can visit increases the more days you buy (eg a four-day ticket allows four extra visits; a five-day ticket allows five).

Days	Multiday Prices (age 10+/age 3-9)	Park Hopper (age 10+/age 3-9)	Park Hopper Plus (age 10+/age 3-9)
2	$202/192	$267/257	$287/277
3	$294/279	$369/354	$389/374
4	$372/356	$447/431	$467/451
5	$390/370	$475/455	$495/475
6	$402/384	$487/469	$507/489
7	$406/392	$491/477	$511/497
8	$424/400	$509/485	$529/505
9	$432/414	$517/499	$537/519
10	$440/420	$525/505	$545/525

impairments, and services for guests who are visually impaired. Sign-language interpreting services require advance reservations.

Business Hours

Bars 4pm to 1am or 2am weekdays, 3am on weekends.

Museums 10am to 5pm.

Nightclubs 9pm to 1am or 2am weekdays, 3am on weekends.

Restaurants Breakfast 7am or 8am to 11am; lunch 11am or 11:30am to 2:30pm or 3pm; dinner 5pm or 6pm to 10pm Sunday to Thursday, to 11pm or midnight Friday and Saturday.

Shops 10am to 7pm Monday to Saturday, noon to 6pm Sunday.

Theme Parks 9am to 6pm, often later; check websites for daily hours.

Discount Cards

Visit Orlando (☏ 407-363-5872; www.visitorlando.com; 8102 International Dr; ☉ 8am-8pm; ☐ I-Ride Trolley Red Line 11) now offers discounts on its website instead of through the Orlando MagiCard. Also keep in mind that Orlando is a *very* competitive tourist destination, so persistence, patience and thorough research often pays dividends.

My Disney Experience: FastPass & MagicBand

FastPass+ is Disney's free ride reservation system, designed to help you plan your visit in advance and reduce waiting times in line. Visitors can reserve a specific time for up to three attractions per day through My Disney Experience (www.disneyworld.com), accessible online or by downloading the free mobile app. There are also kiosks in each park where you can make reservations.

Resort guests receive a **MagicBand** – a plastic wristband that serves as a room key, park entrance ticket, FastPass+ access and room charge. As soon as you make your room reservation, you can set up your My Disney Experience account and begin planning your day-by-day Disney itinerary. A MagicBand will be sent to you in advance or it will be waiting for you when you check into your hotel. Your itinerary, including any changes you make online or through the mobile app, will automatically be stored in your wristband.

Once at the park, head to your reserved FastPass+ ride or attraction anytime within the preselected one-hour timeframe. Go to the FastPass+ entrance, scan your MagicBand and zip right onto the attraction with no more than a 15-minute wait.

Electricity

Type A
120V/60Hz

Type B
120V/60Hz

Health
COVID-19

Orlando and Orange County (like the rest of Florida) have lifted all government mandated COVID restrictions. However, some local businesses continue to operate with reduced hours or services, and some may ask you to wear face coverings indoors. In the theme parks, vaccinations are recommended but not mandatory, and face coverings are optional for all but advised in indoor spaces.

Universal Orlando Resort Tickets

Tickets for the three Universal Orlando Resort Parks (Islands of Adventure, Universal Studios and Volcano Bay) cost the following:

No of Days	One Park ($) adult/child	Two Parks ($) adult/child	Three Parks ($) adult/child
1	119/114 (Volcano Bay 80/75)	174/169	n/a
2	190/185	235/225	310/300
3	n/a	255/245	330/320
4	n/a	265/255	350/340

• Tickets are good anytime within 14 consecutive days, and multiple-day tickets include admission to paid venues in CityWalk. Universal Orlando Resort participates in the Orlando Flex Ticket available online or in person at the Orlando **Official Visitor Center** (☎407-363-5872; www.visitorlando.com; 8102 International Dr; ☺8am-8pm; ☐I-Ride Trolley Red Line 11).

• Avoid lines at designated Islands of Adventure and Universal Studios rides by flashing your Express Pass at the separate Express Pass line. The standard one-day pass (for Islands of Adventure and Universal Studios from $70; for Volcano Bay from $20) allows one-time Express Pass access to each attraction; the unlimited version allows you unlimited access to rides (from $90; Volcano Bay from $40). If you are staying at one of Universal Orlando's deluxe resort hotels – Universal Orlando's Loews Portofino Bay, Hard Rock or Loews Royal Pacific Resort – up to five guests in each room automatically receive an Unlimited Express Pass.

COVID-19 protocols are subject to change. Always check the latest requirements for travel to/within the USA at the CDC website (www.cdc.gov/coronavirus) and www.canitravel.net.

Medical Services

Arnold Palmer Hospital for Children (☎407-649-9111; www.arnoldpalmerhospital.com; 1414 Kuhl Ave; ☺24hr) Orlando's primary children's hospital. Located just east of I-4 at exit 81.

Centra Care Walk-In Medical (☎407-934-2273; www.centracare.org; ☺8am-midnight Mon-Fri, to 8pm Sat & Sun) Walk-in medical center with more than 20 locations.

Doctors on Call Service (DOCS; ☎407-399-3627; www.doctorsoncallservice.com; ☺24hr) Twenty-four-hour doctors on-call to your hotel, including to Walt Disney World® and Universal Orlando Resort.

Dr P Phillips Hospital (☎407-351-8500; www.orlandohealth.com/facilities/dr-p-phillips-hospital;

9400 Turkey Lake Rd; (⏱24hr) Closest hospital to Universal Orlando Resort, SeaWorld and International Drive.

Florida Hospital Celebration Health (Map p40, E8; ☏ 407-303-4000; www.floridahospital.com/celebration-health; 400 Celebration Pl, Kissimmee; (⏱24hr) Closest hospital to Walt Disney World®.

Internet Access

It is not difficult to get connected in Orlando. All theme parks and many sights offer free connection, as do numerous cafes, plus all hotels (though this may be included as part of a 'resort fee').

LGBTIQ+ Travelers

It explodes during **Gay Days** (www.gaydays.com; (⏱Jun), but there is a solid LGBTIQ+ community in Orlando year-round.

Maps

Walt Disney World® Resort

Park maps with listings of the day's scheduled events and activities (including character

meets) are available at the park entrances, Guest Services and all retail locations throughout the parks. Otherwise, the My Disney Experience app has geo-locator maps of every inch of Disney property to help you orient yourself.

Universal Orlando Resort

Pick up a free map at each park entrance (and dotted around at stands within the park). They also list the attractions, with a schedule outlining events, shows and locations of free character interactions. The monthly *Times & Info Guide* lists larger parades and events, too.

Money

You will find ATMs throughout Walt Disney World® and Universal Resort Orlando, though most ATM withdrawals using out-of-state cards incur surcharges of $3 or so. Guest Services at each park offer limited currency exchange. Major credit cards are widely accepted.

Tipping

Tipping is *not* optional. Only withhold tips in cases of outrageously bad service.

Airport skycaps and hotel bellhops $2 per bag, minimum $5 per cart.

Bartenders 10% to 15% per round or $1 per drink.

Concierges Nothing for simple information, up to $20 for securing last-minute restaurant reservations, sold-out show tickets etc.

Housekeeping staff $2 to $4 daily, more if you're messy; sometimes there's an envelope left in the room for this purpose.

Parking valets At least $2 when handed back your car keys.

Restaurant staff and room service 15% to 25%, unless a gratuity is already charged.

Taxi drivers 10% to 15% of metered fare, rounded up to the next dollar.

Safe Travel

Crime Tangelo Park (behind International Dr and Kirkman Rd, not far

Orlando with Young Kids

Families with little ones, loaded down with strollers, car-seats and soft-sided cooler packs, flock to Orlando by the hundreds of thousands every year. The main draw, of course, is the theme parks, and the challenge for parents is digging through the overwhelming options and inflated rhetoric to find what best suits their time, budget and family.

Theme Parks

Ride-through-stories, gentle spins on fanciful creatures and brightly colored splash play areas entertain little ones for hours and days. Children three years and younger don't pay theme-park admission. At Walt Disney World® Resort, Universal Orlando Resort and SeaWorld, baby care centers provide quiet places for nursing and downtime, sell diapers, over-the-counter children's medication and more; some also offer a full kitchen. Look for them on park maps.

Strollers

Strollers (single/double per day $15/31, multiday $13/27) are available on a first-come, first-served basis at Disney's four theme parks and Disney Springs, and you can also purchase umbrella strollers.

Finding the Right Pace

A vacation to central Florida and the theme parks can be exhausting for children and adults alike, and you'd be surprised at how difficult it can be to carve out downtime. Orlando hotels have lazy rivers, toddler-friendly slides and zero-entry pools, beaches and playgrounds. An occasional lazy morning, lunch reservations in an air-conditioned restaurant, and long afternoons at the hotel pool do wonders for everyone's spirits.

from Universal Orlando Resort) and the Orange Blossom Trail (OBT), especially between North Rosemont and Turnpike South, have issues with drugs and crime. The north end of International Dr isn't particularly dangerous, but be on the lookout for petty thievery – where there are tourists there are often pickpockets looking for an easy score.

Heat Summer temperatures soar and bring with them a killer humidity. Stay well hydrated and use a high-SPF sunscreen.

Wildlife Central Florida is home to alligators and snakes, which may be found in some waterways and marshes in residential areas and on golf courses and the like.

Meeting Disney Characters

Folks of all ages pay a lot of money and spend hours in line to get their photo taken with Winnie-the-Pooh, Donald Duck, Elsa and other Disney favorites – Mickey and Minnie are still top of most wish lists. If this is what makes you swoon (versus just spotting them from a short distance, which can also be fun), see www.disneyworld.com. There is a plethora of opportunities to sidle up next to a princess, villain or furry friend.

Disney Character Dining

Make reservations up to six months (yes, six!) for any of the 20 or so **character-dining meals** (☏ 407-939-3463; www.disneyworld.com; Walt Disney World® theme parks & resort hotels; prices vary widely) at Walt Disney World®. They're hardly relaxing and are rather loud and chaotic. Characters stop at each table to pose for a photograph and interact briefly.

Disney's **Grand Floridian Resort** (☏ 407-939-5277; www.disneyworld. com; 4401 Floridian Way) has a buffet breakfast featuring Winnie-the-Pooh, Mary Poppins and Alice in Wonderland, plus it holds the **Perfectly Princess Tea Party**. There's a jam-packed breakfast and dinner with Goofy, Donald Duck and pals at **Chef Mickey's** (p47) in Disney's Contemporary Resort; princesses mingle in Epcot's Norway at the **Akershus Royal Banquet** (p81); and the 100 Acre Wood folk come to Magic Kingdom's **Crystal Palace** (p64) for three meals a day.

At **Cinderella's Royal Table** (p63), Cinderella greets guests and sits for a formal portrait, and a sit-down meal with princesses is served upstairs inside the iconic castle.

Character Spots

Each Walt Disney World® theme park has specific spots where Disney characters hang out, and you can simply hop in line (and wait and wait) to meet them and have your photo taken. A few character spots, such as **Enchanted Tales with Belle**, include a short performance. In addition, check your map and Times Guide for times and locations of scheduled character greetings, and always keep your eyes open – you never know who you'll see!

Campfire Singalong

For something a little different, warm up your pipes at the **Chip 'n' Dale Campfire Singalong** (p49) at Disney's Fort Wilderness Resort.

Hurricanes Hurricane season is between June and November.

Telephone Services

Disney Numbers

Walt Disney World® (📞 407-939-5277) Central number for all things Disney, including packages, tickets, room and dining reservations, and general questions about hours and scheduled events. They'll connect you to anything you need.

Walt Disney World® 'Disney Dining' (📞 407-939-3463) Book priority dining reservations up to 180 days in advance, including character meals, dinner shows and specialty dining. You can also book online or through your My Disney Experience app (www.disneyworld.com).

Walt Disney World® 'Enchanting Extras Collection' (Recreation) (📞 407-939-7529) Horseback riding, boating and more.

Walt Disney World® 'Enchanting Extras Collection' (Tours) (📞 407-939-8687) Tours at all of Disney's four theme parks. One of these gives a 'behind the scenes' look; excellent for return visitors.

Walt Disney World® 'Theme Parks Lost & Found' (📞 407-824-4245) Items are sent to this central location at the end of each day; also see Guest Services at individual parks.

Universal Orlando Resort Numbers

Dining CityWalk & Theme Parks (📞 407-224-9255) Advanced priority seating for CityWalk, Islands of Adventure and Universal Studios.

Dining Resort Hotels (📞 407-503-3463) Advanced priority seating for Loews Portofino Bay, Hard Rock and Loews Royal Pacific Resorts.

Guest Services (📞 407-224-6350, 407-244-4233)

Resort Hotel Reservations (📞 888-

273-1311, for vacation packages 📞 888-343-3636) Accommodations at Universal's on-site resort hotels.

Universal Orlando Resort (📞 407-363-8000, toll-free 📞 800-232-7827) Central number for all things Universal (although infuriatingly automated).

Universal Orlando Resort Lost & Found (📞 407-224-4233) Located inside Guest Services.

Tourist Information

Official Visitor Center – Visit Orlando (📞 407-363-5872; www.visitorlando.com; 8102 International Dr; ⏰ 8am-8pm; 🚋 I-Ride Trolley Red Line 11) The best source for information on theme parks, accommodations, outdoor activities, performing arts and more.

Orlando Informer (www.orlandoinformer.com) Excellent and detailed information on all things Universal, including park changes, money-saving tips, menus and a crowd calendar.

Universal Orlando Resort (www.universal orlando.com) Official site for information, accommodations and tickets.

Visas & Entry Requirements

Visitors from the UK, Australia, New Zealand, Japan and many EU countries don't need visas for stays of less than 90 days, though they must get approval from the Electronic System for Travel Authorization (ESTA). Visitors from Canada need neither a visa nor ESTA approval for stays of less than 90 days. Citizens of other nations should check http://travel.state.gov.

Non-US citizens 18 and older must show proof that they are fully vaccinated with an accepted COVID-19 vaccine before boarding a plane to the USA.

Responsible Travel

In the Theme Parks

Electric trams, solar power and enhanced recycling and conservation programs are just some of the ways the theme parks are trying to be greener. Universal Orlando is even compacting refuse from 30 of its restaurants and transforming it into fuel.

Public Transportation

Orlando has one of the best public transportation systems in the state, including a growing fleet of electric buses. The major theme parks also operate an extensive transportation network, ferrying guests between their parks and many of their hotels.

Renewable Energy

Orlando was the first city in Florida to require public disclosure of energy and water efficiency in buildings and is on course toward achieving its goal of 100% renewable energy city-wide by 2050.

Green Lodging Program

Ninety-five hotels in the Orlando area (including 36 on I-Drive) are included in Florida's Green Lodging Program, a four-tiered award system that recognises efforts in water conservation, recycling, energy efficiency and indoor air quality.

Urban Farm Programs

Many restaurants in Downtown and Winter Park participate in urban farm programs that result in local produce on menus.

Behind the Scenes

Send Us Your Feedback

We love to hear from travelers – your comments help make our books better. We read every word, and we guarantee that your feedback goes straight to the authors. Visit **lonelyplanet.com/contact** to submit your updates and suggestions.

Note: We may edit, reproduce and incorporate your comments in Lonely Planet products such as guidebooks, websites and digital products, so let us know if you don't want your comments reproduced or your name acknowledged. For a copy of our privacy policy visit lonelyplanet.com/legal.

Fionn's Thanks

A huge thanks to Kevin Gibson and Jon Hornbuckle at Universal Orlando; to the Disney gang – Priya, Charlotte, Dave and Nikki; to Diane and Lisa at SeaWorld; to Margaret Henriksson; and to Amy Rodenbrock, Paula Ramirez and Jo Cooke of Visit Orlando. A big thanks to Dyna Stephens for being a terrific landlady, and to Vicky Smith at Lonely Planet for being there every step of the way through this update. And finally, a big thanks to my wife Laura for being ok with my being away for a whole month!

Acknowledgements

This Book

This 3rd edition of Lonely Planet's *Pocket Orlando & Walt Disney World® Resort* guidebook was researched and written by Fionn Davenport. This guidebook was produced by the following:

Commissioning Editors
Victoria Smith, Kirsten Rawlings

Regional Senior Cartographer Alison Lyall

Product Editor
Saralinda Turner

Book Designer
Ania Lenihan

Assisting Editors
Michelle Bennett, Melanie Dankel, Barbara Delissen

Cover Researchers
Gwen Cotter, Brendan Dempsey-Spencer

Thanks to Karen Henderson, Sonia Kapoor, Max Magura

Index

See also separate subindexes for:

- ✱ **Eating** p174
- ◉ **Drinking** p175
- ✪ **Entertainment** p175
- 🔒 **Shopping** p175

Index

Sights 000
Map Pages **000**

Index

Our Writer

Fionn Davenport

Irish by birth and conviction, Fionn has spent the last two decades focusing on the country of his birth and its nearest neighbor, England. He's written extensively for Lonely Planet and contributed oodles of travel pieces to a host of newspapers and magazines including the *Irish Times*, *Irish Independent*, *Irish Daily Mail*, *Lonely Planet Magazine*, *Cara*, the *Independent* and the *Daily Telegraph*.

Published by Lonely Planet Global Limited
CRN 554153
3rd edition – Dec 2022
ISBN 978 1 78701 747 4
© Lonely Planet 2022   Photographs © as indicated 2022
10 9 8 7 6 5 4 3 2 1
Printed in Singapore